A RICH DAD ADVISOR BOOK

VEIL NOT FAIL

PROTECTING YOUR PERSONAL ASSETS FROM BUSINESS ATTACKS

GARRETT SUTTON, ESQ.

FOREWORD BY ROBERT KIYOSAKI

A RICH DAD ADVISOR BOOK

VEIL NOT FAIL

PROTECTING YOUR PERSONAL ASSETS FROM BUSINESS ATTACKS

GARRETT SUTTON, ESQ.

FOREWORD BY ROBERT KIYOSAKI

If you purchase this book without a cover you should be aware that this book may have been stolen property and reported as "unsold and destroyed" to the publisher. In such case neither the author nor the publisher has received any payment for this "stripped book."

This publication is designed to provide competent and reliable information regarding the subject matter covered. However, it is sold with the understanding that the author and publisher are not engaged in rendering legal, financial, or other professional advice. Laws and practices often vary from state to state and country to country and if legal or other expert assistance is required, the services of a professional should be sought. The author and publisher specifically disclaim any liability that is incurred from the use or application of the contents of this book.

Copyright ©2022 by Garrett Sutton, Esq. All rights reserved. Except as permitted under the U.S. Copyright Act of 1976, no part of this publication may be reproduced, distributed, or transmitted in any form or by any means or stored in a database or retrieval system, without the prior written permission of the publisher.

Published by RDA Press, LLC

Rich Dad Advisors, B-I Triangle, CASHFLOW Quadrant and other Rich Dad marks are registered trademarks of CASHFLOW Technologies, Inc.

RDA Press LLC
15170 N. Hayden Road
Scottsdale, AZ 85260
480-998-5400

Visit our Web sites: RDA-Press.com and CorporateDirect.com

Printed in Canada

ISBN: 978-1-947588-16-5

042022

Read The Book That Started It All

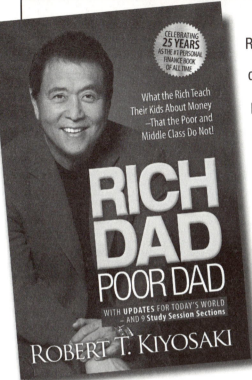

Robert Kiyosaki has challenged and changed the way tens of millions of people around the world think about money. With perspectives that often contradict conventional wisdom, Robert has earned a reputation for straight talk, irreverence and courage. He is regarded worldwide as a passionate advocate for financial education.

Rich Dad Poor Dad will...

- Explode the myth that you need to earn a high income to become rich
- Challenge the belief that your house is an asset
- Show parents why they can't rely on the school system to teach their kids about money
- Define once and for all an asset and a liability
- Teach you what to teach your kids about money for their future financial success

Rich Dad Poor Dad — The #1 Personal Finance Book of All Time!

Order your copy at
richdad.com today!

Best-Selling Books in the Rich Dad Advisors Series

BY BLAIR SINGER

Sales Dogs
You Don't Have to Be an Attack Dog to Explode Your Income

Team Code of Honor
The Secrets of Champions in Business and in Life

Summit Leadership
Taking Your Team to the Top

BY GARRETT SUTTON, ESQ.

Start Your Own Corporation
Why the Rich Own their Own Companies and Everyone Else Works for Them

Writing Winning Business Plans
How to Prepare a Business Plan that Investors will Want to Read and Invest In

Buying and Selling a Business
How You Can Win in the Business Quadrant

The ABCs of Getting Out of Debt
Turn Bad Debt into Good Debt and Bad Credit into Good Credit

Run Your Own Corporation
How to Legally Operate and Properly Maintain Your Company into the Future

The Loopholes of Real Estate
Secrets of Successful Real Estate Investing

Scam-Proof Your Assets
Guarding Against Widespread Deception

Veil Not Fail
Protecting Your Personal Assets from Business Attacks

BY KEN MCELROY

ABCs of Real Estate Investing
The Secrets of Finding Hidden Profits Most Investors Miss

ABCs of Property Management
What You Need to Know to Maximize Your Money Now

ABCs of Advanced Real Estate Investing
How to Identify the Hottest Markets and Secure the Best Deals

ABCs of Buying Rental Property
How You Can Achieve Financial Freedom in Five Years

ABCs of Raising Capital
Only Lazy People Use their Own Money

BY TOM WHEELWRIGHT

Tax-Free Wealth
How to Build Massive Wealth by Permanently Lowering Your Taxes

BY ANDY TANNER

Stock Market Cash Flow
Four Pillars of Investing for Thriving in Today's Markets

BY JOSH AND LISA LANNON

The Social Capitalist
Passion and Profits – An Entrepreneurial Journey

Contents

Foreword	by Robert Kiyosaki	*xi*
Introduction		*xiii*
Chapter One	The Most Painful Piercing in History	1
Chapter Two	They Can't Take My Assets, Can They?	7
Chapter Three	How Did Limited Liability Evolve?	23
Chapter Four	How Can a Corporate Veil be Pierced?	29
Chapter Five	A Quick Summary	41
Chapter Six	The Fredo Case – Breach of Fiduciary Duties	45
Chapter Seven	Corporate Opportunities Entitled Officers – Angry Shareholders	53
Chapter Eight	Bull's–eye on Business Judgment	61
Chapter Nine	The Wallop Case – Self Dealing?	69
Chapter Ten	Summary Judgement – Getting out Quick	79
Chapter Eleven	Internal Affairs: Which State's Law Applies?	85
Chapter Twelve	Clark Kent at Fault	93
Chapter Thirteen	Two Companies – One Owner A Bull's–eye or a Miss?	99
Chapter Fourteen	The Communist Takeover Case	105

Chapter Fifteen	The Wizard of Oz in Connecticut	109
Chapter Sixteen	Undercapitalization	117
Chapter Seventeen	Reverse Veil Piercing	127
Chapter Eighteen	Wife vs. Husband. Husband vs. Wife.	133
Chapter Nineteen	All in the Family Liability: Parent-Child, Sister Frankenstein	137
Chapter Twenty	Dissolve and Run?	141
Chapter Twenty-One	The Government Piercith	153
Chapter Twenty-Two	Piercing Around the World	157
Chapter Twenty-Three	Maintaining Corporate Formalities	165
Chapter Twenty-Four	How to Stay Protected	183
Appendix A	The Law of Fraudulent Transfers	193
Appendix B	Nevada Fiduciary Law	209
Appendix C	Corporate Dissolution Statutes of Limitation	213
Appendix D	The Laya Factors Laya v. Erin Homes, Inc. 177 W. Va. 343 (1986)	223
Foot Notes		227
Index		233

Foreword
by Robert Kiyosaki

How would you feel if you were standing in a courtroom, in front of a judge, and only then found out that your attorney was incompetent? A judge delivering the body blow that your attorney failed to protect your assets... on a minor technicality.

Your opponent, the person who is suing you, smiles and shouts, *"Hallelujah. What you once owned, is now mine!"*

Garrett Sutton is my personal asset protection attorney. Without Garrett protecting my assets, everything I worked to amass over a lifetime would be gone.

I have been that person, the one who's been sued, standing in a courtroom watching the opposing attorney searching for any little technicality that would "pierce the corporate veil" — any opening or opportunity to get at my personal assets.

As an old saying goes: *"Sometimes, it's the little things that count the most."*

Sometimes the risk of missing the minutiae falls squarely on your shoulders. Maybe you told your attorney that you'd take care of the continuing obligations to keep your LLC or corporation current. Or, worse yet, maybe you set up the entity yourself and don't even know that there are more rules to follow to stay protected.

In these cases, you can't blame anyone but yourself. And here's the thing: These rules are very easy to follow. But if you don't pay attention to them — if you are lazy or ignorant of the rules and what's required of you — you can lose everything.

I endorse Garrett's book *Veil Not Fail* because he is the type of legal professional that his clients can count on to advise them of all the points and processes for keeping a legal entity in good standing so that it delivers the maximum asset protection. If you have anything worth protecting, all of Garrett's books may prove priceless.

Take it from me — once you get to court, it's the little things that count the most. Use Garrett's experience and guidance... to stay out of court.

Robert Kiyosaki

Introduction

Protecting your personal assets from business attacks requires the strategic use of corporate law.

Your key safeguard is the 'corporate veil,' which is discussed throughout this book and which, if not properly maintained, can lead to devastating personal losses.

Veils do fail. Their protection is at your election.

Traditionally, a veil is a piece of opaque or transparent material worn over one's face for concealment or protection from the elements. A veil is not as strong as an iron helmet worn into battle. You have to be much more careful with a veil. In the business world a veil is what separates the individual from their company's operations. This corporate veil offers some protection but, as before, it is transparent and neither rigid nor thick. People suing your business can see (or with some small effort can learn) who is behind the veil. And if the business can't pay their debts a claimant can try and lift the veil to get at the individual assets of the person behind the veil.

Piercing the corporate veil (which applies to LLCs and LPs as well) is an important strategy. For plaintiffs (the people suing) seeking collection from a company without assets it is a way to collect from the individual owners of the business. For those same owners who don't want to be held personally responsible for the debts of their business it is a critical defensive strategy. You want the veil of protection to always be strong and protect you from outside attacks.

To stay protected you must follow the rules, often called 'corporate formalities.' If you don't follow them (and many people don't) your veil will fail.

Let's consider a second way to explain it: Your business has a bull's-eye on it.

xiii

That red center amid outwardly concentric circles is the target in archery, riflery and business litigation. Shooting at targets with arrows and bullets can be competitive and satisfying. In a business context it can mean losing everything you own.

Most business owners and asset investors (in real estate, stocks, bonds, bullion, crypto and the like) know that they need protection. As I have written in *Start Your Own Corporation, Run Your Own Corporation*, and *Loopholes of Real Estate*, among other books, we live in a litigious society. People sue each other all the time, and you and I are not going to change that system. So, we have to work within it. The system allows us to set up corporations, limited liability companies (LLCs) and limited partnerships (LPs), collectively "entities", for protection. But the system also requires that we properly maintain those entities for ongoing protection.

Which is why the bull's-eye is always on your business. If you don't follow the requirements, the 'corporate formalities', a business claimant can hit the bull's-eye and pierce through the entity to reach your personal assets. When the plaintiff hits the bright red center target, which is always there despite all of your best efforts, they can get at everything you own.

Imagine piercing the veil in terms of a very expensive science fiction movie. On the trillion- dollar space ship there is, incredibly enough, one little speck of a spot of compromise that, if things cosmically fall into place with the exact shot, can jeopardize the entire fleet. If the insurgents can somehow, against all odds, hit that well defended bull's-eye, the galaxy will be saved.

Piercing the veil isn't that hard on Earth. It happens in almost 50% of cases. People forget the bull's-eye is always on their business, they forget to follow all the corporate formalities and then they unforgettably lose everything when the veil is pierced.

Hitting the bull's-eye and piercing the veil is heavily dependent on the specific facts in each case. As such, we will be reviewing a number of interesting cases in the field. Since some who have lost in court would probably rather forget about it, we have somewhat disguised their names. While the court reports are a matter of public record, we have changed the names out of courtesy and not any legal obligation. We have also altered the names in the court reporting as well and hopefully the judges and their clerks will understand our rationale. However, in cases involving public figures, including US Senator Malcolm Wallop and billionaire George Soros, as well as those darned Communists, we have used the names of actual parties to better flesh out the specifics of each case.

In most of the cases we have been brief and to the point, as in this is what the court said and why it's important. But in a few cases, such as the Compre and Purdom conflicts in Chapter 20, we have provided the complete procedural history, the back and forth between attorneys and the court. As you read these cases think of all the attorney's fees involved. We're not mentioning this to boil your blood. Instead, appreciate that when an attorney takes on a case that goes to court, they now have a duty to their client, you, to fight it the right way. Everything is public record at this point. And everything can be reviewed for lapses and error. If your attorney doesn't properly engage in the procedural back and forth they can be held liable for legal malpractice, a failure to represent you according to very strict professional standards. But that duty also makes things pretty expensive. So in reading these cases, understand the attorney's fraught position. He or she has a duty to represent you to the fullest which, with all the required back and forth, is going to cost you alot in fees.

At the same time, consider that the case never arose in the first place. Imagine that all the corporate formalities were followed (and they're not hard to follow) and no one is trying to pierce your veil. Imagine that you did a credit check on a client and decided, given their weak standing, simply not to do business with them. Many of the cases herein, and out there, with early prudence would never have landed in an expensive court room. And that's why we wrote this book. To keep you out of the financial and very emotional crush of litigation. The bull's–eye is always there, but you will now learn how to better defend yourself and, even better, never have a claim brought against you searching for (and even reaching) your personal assets.

Veil piercing, like America itself, extends all the way back to the American Revolution...

Chapter One

The Most Painful Piercing in History

December 1, 1772

"I despise my Americans. They won't pay for a thing!"

King George III was livid. Maintaining his North American colonies cost a fortune. And the beneficiaries of his magnificence wouldn't pay a pence for defense.

"You have a much better deal with us," said Owen Clive, the head of Britain's East India Company. "You grant us the rights to India, we take care of all administrative and military costs and you share in the profits."

"No one can know about that," said the King.

"Of course not, Your Majesty," said Clive, noting to himself that everyone did. "What if we worked out a way for our Company to solve your American problem?"

George the Third, thirty-four years old and set on showing the world who was in charge, looked Clive in the eye. "How?"

"In a word: Tea."

"Go on," said the King.

"Tea is expensive in the colonies, with all the outbound British tariffs. The French, Danes and Dutch get the tea to American smugglers to avoid your taxes but it still is an expensive commodity. As you know, we now have a huge surplus of tea here in London."

"Because of your famine."[1]

1

Chapter One

"It's not really our famine," said Clive, referring to the 10 million Bengalis who died of starvation in 1770. "You can blame the local landlords if you please."

"I don't study mercantile matters," said the King. "But it seems that losing 10 million tea drinkers would be bad for business."

"We do have a surplus," said Clive. "So, what if in your great way we could sell our tea and put down your Americans at the same time?"

"Let me think about that," said King George.

Clive paused and then said, "I see where you're going, Your Majesty."

"You do?"

"Yes," said Clive, "you're thinking that if we sold our excess tea in America for a low price and added on a small tax, we could gain the upper hand."

"Yes," said the King. "I was thinking that. Please explain it further."

"The Americans hate it when we tax them at home. But they like their tea. So, we have a very small tax on the tea that's sold in America. The tea is sold at a discount so we gain control of the market. We get the Americans used to paying local taxes and gradually raise them. The East India Company, like we've done in India, in due course takes over the American economy."

"And I get a share of that," said the King.

"Of course, you do," said Clive. "You keep the taxes and get a share of East India's profits."

"The Americans have been short changing my revenues for too long. They're all a bunch of criminals."

"Yes, Your Majesty," said Clive. "Granted you have been saving the government a lot of money by emptying out the prisons here and sending all the felons to Baltimore."

"Yes," said the King blithely. "What better way to harass the Catholics?"

"However, the highway men have now spread throughout the colonies. Felons are everywhere in America."

"Everyone knows it's part penal colony," said the King dismissively. He then paused. "But you're right. All those wretched smugglers have reduced my tariff take."

2

The Most Painful Piercing in History

"And that is the beauty of your plan, Your Majesty. The low prices will put all the smugglers out of business."

The King smiled. "You know, we prohibit 26 types of commercial activities in the colonies."

"I know, Your Majesty. The London merchants love your restrictions on American manufacturing. What if the East India Company controlled those industries within America? Just like we do in India."

"A fortune," said the King. "An absolute fortune! I'd have serfs again! Vassal serfs I can tax to the hilt." The King looked at Clive. "But no one can know about this. I can't lose a thing in this grab."

"Certainly not," said Clive. "The East India Company is a chartered corporation. Your liability is limited to your investment, which is minimal. And if the company ever gets in trouble—"

"Which it does every decade," said the King.

"Now and then," said Clive. "But if it does you are personally protected by the corporate veil. No one would dare pierce the veil to get at the King's assets."

"I've got the finest military on earth to prevent that."

"You certainly do," said Clive. "You've done a wonderful job at that."

"Thank you," said the King.

"Shall we get started?" said Clive.

"Make it so," said King George the Third.

June 4, 1773

Benjamin Franklin was in London attending Parliament as an American observer. Noting that the large duty on East India Company tea would be removed in Britain and a small duty would be imposed in America, Franklin wrote:

> ...The 'wise' scheme is, to take off so much duty here as will make tea cheaper in America than foreigners can supply us and to confine the duty there, (in America) to keep up the exercise of the right. They have no idea, that any people can act from any other

3

principle but that of self-interest; and they believe that 3d. on a pound of tea, of which one does not drink perhaps ten pounds in a year, is sufficient to overcome all the patriotism of an American.[2]

Soon, letters and handbills in opposition circulated the colonies. In town meetings citizens declared that the duty, however small, established a local taxing power and affixed the badge of slavery. In New York, 'The Alarm No. 1' handbill warned of the East India Company's monopoly power in India being injected into America.[3]

In Philadelphia a handbill was addressed to "Tradesmen and Mechanics of Pennsylvania." It described the East India Company's "career of bloodshed and plunder in India and predicted an unhappy fate for America if the greedy corporation was allowed to obtain a foothold."[4]

The opposition grew. "The idea that there was a deep-laid plot against America is pushed to its fullest extent in one of Hamilton's productions. The present minister in conjunction with a mercenary tribe of merchants, attempted to effect by stratagem, what could not be done by an open undisguised manner of proceeding. His emissaries, everywhere, were set to work. They endeavored by every possible device to allure us into the snare. The act, passed for the purpose, was misrepresented; and we were assured, with all the parade of pretended patriotism, that our liberties were in no danger. The advantage we should receive from the probable cheapness of English tea was played off with every exaggeration of falsehood, and specious declamations on the criminality of illicit trade served as a gilding for the whole."[5]

Voices were united in opposition to the East India Company. Protestors argued that the East India Company and King George were alter egos of each other, that they were one in the same and united in tyranny.

At loud and vocal gatherings, potential agents for the East India Company in Philadelphia and New York were warned not to take the tea. Under pressure, the agents resigned and the ships, without unloading the tea, were sent back to Britain.

In Charleston, the tea was unloaded but no one would purchase it. The tea finally spoiled.

The Most Painful Piercing in History

In Boston the agents didn't resign and the tea was brought into port. On December 16, 1773 the Boston Tea Party erupted. The entire shipment of East India Company tea was thrown overboard and destroyed in the sea water. The British responded harshly to this act of rebellion and the American Revolution was on.

September 5, 1783

King George III was livid. "We just signed the Treaty of Paris with those bloody Americans. They gained their independence from me!"

"Yes, Your Majesty," said Clive.

"You said the East India Company's corporate veil would protect me!"

"Right," said Clive, "that's right. But sometimes, well, the veil is pierced—"

"Veils are pierced when your Company crosses the line!" yelled the King. "Now I have to find a new penal colony."

"We have some ideas for that," said Clive. "We've sighted a large island in the South Seas-"

"Not so fast," said the King. "Back to this: The Americans pierced through your Company and took my assets."

"Your assets, sir?"

"They're gone! My dominion of one million square miles of land, buildings and improvements. All lost! Those criminals took all my North American real estate."

"You still have Canada, Your Majesty."

"Like that's any consolation." The King glared at the CEO. "How do you explain what happened?"

Clive was silent for a moment. "I suppose Americans don't like large corporations."

"No," said the King. "Americans don't like large corporations manipulating their affairs."

The greatest piercing in history – King George III's loss of the American colonies – provides lessons for all owners of corporations and LLCs.

Chapter One

The rules of good governance must be followed to protect a corporate veil. A company must not act as a mere extension of its owners. The organization, dare we say, must be independent.

In the pages ahead we will discuss how you can master this key business strategy – maintaining a strong corporate veil so that your personal assets stay protected. We shall not forget that the bull's–eye is always on your business and asset holdings, and that constant vigilance is required to stay protected in our highly litigious society.

Chapter Two

They Can't Take My Assets, Can They?

You dreamed of running your own business — and now you do.

You purchased a small home and turned it into a rental property. You appreciate that renting out real estate does constitute a business and you've got a couple of successful years under your belt. You're feeling confident.

From the beginning, you tried to do everything right.

You created a single-member limited liability company, Great Expectations, LLC, to protect your personal assets. You printed up business cards but left off the "LLC" at the end of your business name because that sounded too officious. You opened a business checking account and obtained an Employer Identification Number, which you need to file your taxes and hire employees.

Your cash flow isn't always as high as you would like, so you often use your personal account to cover the bills. You're supposed to file a state annual report on your LLC, but you have been too busy to do that. No one reads that stuff anyway, you reason. The most important thing is that you're paying the bills and earning equity on your property. Your financial situation is improving.

But then disaster strikes.

A woman named Amelia trips on a crack in the sidewalk leading to your property and breaks her back. She files a personal injury lawsuit against you and your LLC. You feel empathy for Amelia, but you don't feel responsible for her injury.

Chapter Two

The court disagrees and grants $2 million in damages to Amelia. You only have $300,000 in liability insurance. Your LLC must file for bankruptcy.

But you feel safe because you created Great Expectations, LLC. Injured Amelia can take the equity in your rental property but not the money in your personal bank accounts, or in your home, car or other possessions. After all, that's why you created an LLC — to protect your personal assets. Right?

But Amelia's attorney files a motion with the court aiming at your bull's-eye and seeking to invalidate your veil. You're confused. You thought the veil always protected your personal assets.

Your attorney clarifies the situation by drawing out two charts:

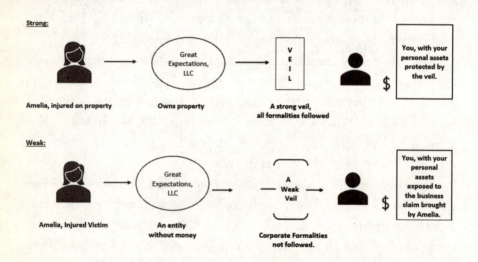

In the first example the corporate formalities have been followed and the veil is strong, protecting your personal assets from business attacks. However, in the second chart, the formalities are lacking, resulting in the great misfortune of personal liability.

This can't happen, you argue.

Your attorney sets you straight. It can and it does.

They Can't Take My Assets, Can They?

In fact, nearly half of all veil-piercing lawsuits filed against small corporations and LLCs (three members or less) are successful, which means your creditors can go after your personal assets. In almost all of those cases, the owner of the LLC failed to follow some simple rules for governing the business and engaged in misleading activity to avoid paying debts. The rules include, but are not limited to, the following:

1. Never mix personal and business monies.
2. Always file paperwork required by state or federal law.
3. Conduct an annual meeting at least once a year.
4. Always use or include the "LLC", "LP" or "Inc." when referring to your company.
5. Never engage in fraudulent or illegal activities.

You didn't violate No. 5. You're a good, honest person.

But your rental investment business didn't follow the first four rules, and fraud is not a necessary condition in tort cases, such as the liability case mentioned above.

Violating the other four rules doesn't mean a court of law will automatically pierce your business's veil. But the more rules you break, the greater the likelihood your LLC won't be able to protect your personal assets. When there is no distinction between you and your business, your business is said to be your alter ego. When the distinction between you and your business blurs, there may be no protection for your personal assets. Your veil will have failed.

Many business people who create LLCs or other closely held (small, privately owned) companies are unfamiliar with these rules. Some have not even heard of the phrase, "piercing the veil."

But, as in our sci-fi movie example, when your insurgent claimant hits that bull's-eye all sorts of calamity can arise within your own personal galaxy.

As a business person, you must protect your veil. Not only for yourself but for your other partners and family members. Mistakes on your part can harm others.

Chapter Two

The purpose of this book is to teach you how to avoid this harm. The bull's–eye is always there. Fortunately, protecting your veil does not involve a lot of work or cost a lot of money. A couple of hours reading this book should give you everything you need and, if you need more, consult with an attorney. Please know that we will often use the term 'corporation' in a way that collectively refers to all entities, be they corporations, LLCs or Limited Partnerships. All three entities can have their veils pierced.

In this chapter we will further define the concepts "corporation" and "corporate veil" and provide some background about piercing.

Although the main focus of this book is on showing you how to protect your company, you also may benefit from piercing if you need to collect a debt from another closely held company. You may want to target their bull's–eye, and pierce their veil to obtain payment. And, if an individual owes you money and owns a closely held business, you can, under some circumstances, file a claim for reverse piercing, which means you can force their company to pay the individual's debt. We will cover reverse piercing in Chapter 17.

What Is a Corporation?

The term "corporate" comes from the Latin word corporatus, which means "to form into a body." Some histories credit Plutarch Numa Pompilius, the second King of Rome, who ruled from 715- 633 B.C., with inventing both the corporate form of organization and the doctrine of limited liability. (You knew it would be the Romans.) The king appears to have originated the idea of separating the individual from the organization. During his reign, schools of learning, religious organizations, and artisan groups all had de facto limited liability. In other words, the teachers, priests and artisans that occupied these societies enjoyed immunity from creditors — and the organization, not its members, was responsible for its debts.

Many years later Rome created a mechanism for protecting some of its citizens from debt collectors. It was called a perculium. A wealthy owner, for example, could set aside some money or property to be used to purchase goods or services and give one of his servants control over the capital. If debts exceeded the capital, the debtor could not seek payment from the servant's owner.

Various forms of limited liability also were extended to public works projects to fund the building of bridges, ports or viaducts. Usually, the state or monarch would grant investors sovereign immunity (limited liability) until the project or funding was completed.

But the doctrine of limited liability had limited influence on the economies of Europe until the Middle Ages, when international shipping grew rapidly in response to increasing population and trade. From the year 1000 to 1500, the population of Europe nearly doubled, going from 57 million to 91 million. Demand for imported goods and raw materials soared, which in turn required more capital to build ships and fund expeditions.

To generate capital, a new type of contract was created: The Commenda. A passive investor known as a commendator would provide capital to a tractator, who hired a captain and a crew for a sea voyage to a foreign land or port to forage or negotiate for goods and raw materials. When the ship returned, the profits were divided up according to an agreed upon ratio. This arrangement is similar to today's limited partnership. Limited liability was extended to commendators, who, like limited partners, had little control over the venture. The tractator, with all the power, acted as the general partner.

Reducing the risk to the investor also meant reducing the cost of the capital to the tractator, which in turn stimulated even more trade.

Back to defining a corporation. For our purposes, a corporation is an association of individuals, empowered by law, that exists independent of its members and is endowed with various legal rights, duties and privileges. A corporation has the legal right to sue, a duty to keep formal records of its business, and the privilege of offering its owners or shareholders limited liability (with some exceptions, of course).

For-profit joint-stock companies first appeared in England in the 16th century. Limited liability was not a feature. Instead, the big advantage of a joint-stock company was that ownership could be easily transferred

Chapter Two

between people through the sale of stock. The British Crown granted these companies monopolies for shipping goods between ports in Europe, Africa, India, Asia and Colonial America. The notorious East India Company, created in 1600 by royal decree, became the world's most powerful (and detested) joint-stock company, eventually ruling a fifth of the world's population with its own army of a quarter of a million soldiers.

In 1612, the Dutch East India Company became the first for-profit organization to offer limited liability to its shareholders. But the idea took some time to catch on in the United Kingdom and the United States, even though it was a very effective way of accumulating capital for investment.

In America before the revolution, resentment against British rule was increasing in part because the corporations that ran the original colonies were mostly fiscally repressive. They would ship raw materials from America to Britain, use them to manufacture finished goods, which were then shipped back to America and sold at extremely high prices. Certain manufacturing activities were prohibited in America, richly benefiting British business owners even more.

In 1776, when the Declaration of Independence was signed, English scholar Adam Smith published *Wealth of Nations*, which argued that competition was the key to keeping greed in check. Smith, though, was no advocate of large-scale corporations, because he believed they hindered competition: "The pretense that corporations are necessary to the better government of the trade is without foundation."

After independence, many American communities created corporations to raise money (sometimes through lotteries) for public works projects, such as digging canals and building bridges. Their charters ended when the project was completed or paid off.

In Britain, however, the East India Company carried on. By the 1700s British consumers discovered desirable Chinese luxury items, such as silks, porcelains and teas. The market for Chinese imports accelerated. But the Qing dynasty ruling China didn't want British manufactured goods in return. Without an exchange in trade the British had to pay the Qing in cash – specifically, silver. Soon there was a large trade imbalance the Brits were keen to avoid. How could they turn things around?

In a word: Opium.

The East India Company, as we've discussed, controlled India and had their own military forces to maintain their order. The Company grew poppies in Bengal, and the opium from their Indian poppies was much stronger than the Chinese version. While opium was illegal in China it was an acceptable exchange for local Chinese traders. In this way the East India Company traded opium for fine Chinese luxury items. Soon the balance of trade was equaled and then solidly in Britain's favor. However, a very big problem became clear. By the 1830's over 80% of all young males along China's east coast were opium addicts. Losing out on the Americans' unwillingness to pay a tea tax fifty years earlier was a big setback for the East India Company. But now they had millions of Chinese hooked on their opium. It was a bonanza and the East India Company was not going to give up the huge profits.

By 1839, the Chinese had had enough of Britain's illegal drug smuggling. The youth of their nation were being sucked into a gutter of opium dependency. The emperor appointed a new governor for Guangzhou, Lin Zexu, to deal sternly with Britain's East India Company and other smugglers. Lin confiscated 42,000 opium pipes and 3 million pounds of opium worth a fortune from British smugglers. In an act eerily similar to the Boston Tea Party, he ordered the opium placed in trenches and drenched in sea water to destroy the valuable commodity.

Once again, the East India Company and the British government reacted harshly and the First Opium War (1839-42) was fought. The British easily defeated Chinese forces and as spoils received Hong Kong island and the right to addict millions more Chinese on their powerful Indian-grown opium.

At the same time, the East India Company was not gaining in popularity in India, which they governed under the guise of British rule. The Indian Rebellion of 1857 resulted in widespread losses as locals fought the Company's rigid colonial governance. The carnage was not pretty.

At this point, the British Crown had had enough of a private company getting its government into wars. In 1858, the British Government nationalized the East India Company and took over all of its possessions

Chapter Two

and military forces. The Company was finally dissolved sixteen years later with a final dividend payment to its owners. As the Times of London wrote of the East India Company on April 8, 1873: "It accomplished a work such as in the whole history of the human race no other trading company ever attempted, and such as none, surely, is likely to attempt in the years to come."

It will be interesting to see if our giant tech companies can equal or exceed the East India Company's audacious societal control.

As part of the East India Company reform, Britain allowed its citizens to create limited liability entities without the need to obtain formal government permission. In the United States, certain states introduced these reforms even earlier. The state of New York was the earliest adopter of protective corporate laws, and their economy boomed. Other states took notice and followed suit.

It is interesting to note that in the United States, corporations are chartered through each of the 50 states, not the federal government. In most countries around the world, national governments regulate the creation and operation of corporations and LLCs. However, after the Revolution, many of the framers of the Constitution wanted to keep a closer, more local check on corporations and so that power was given to each state. As well, at the start of the republic, the framers did not want to grant constitutional protections to corporations.

They had just defeated Britian's nefarious East India Company. Why give large corporations any protection at all? So, as an example, the 4th Amendment prohibits unreasonable searches and seizures against persons. Corporations were not mentioned. Likewise, the 14th Amendment ratified in 1868, dictated that "No state shall deprive any person of life, liberty or property." Corporations were left out again.

However, corporations grew in power and in 1886 the U.S. Supreme Court recognized the corporation as a "natural person" for purposes of the 14th Amendment. [6]

That decision laid the foundation for the 2010 U.S. Supreme Court decision in *Citizens United v. Federal Election Commission*[7] which held that the First Amendment prohibits the government from restricting independent expenditures for political communications by corporations, including for-profit and nonprofit corporations.

But the original effects of the American Revolution are still felt and the good thing about each of the 50 states having their own corporate law is that some states compete against each other to have the most favorable law. Wyoming, Nevada and Delaware are at the forefront of this competition, which works to all of our benefit.

While each country has their own specific rules on the limits of corporate power, corporations everywhere share three common elements.

Three Elements of Corporations

The three elements are: (1) corporate separateness, (2) entity shielding, and (3) limited liability.

1. Corporate Separateness

When people form a corporation, they create a new legal identity separate from themselves and other identities in society. Corporate entities are "legal persons." While they don't breathe or take a walk around the block, they do have the legal capacity to conduct business operations and enter into contracts. People create them to facilitate the production of goods and services or achieve other goals, and to protect individuals from claims against the business. People create them for the veil of protection.

A good example of corporate separateness is illustrated by an incident in 1908 when a developer tried to keep blacks and people of color from buying lots in his Virginia development. Each deed contained a covenant preventing persons of African descent or colored persons from taking title to the lots. To challenge this discrimination, a group of black people created a corporation and purchased some of the lots. A white landowner near the purchased property filed a lawsuit to have the sales canceled. But the court ruled in favor of the corporation, pointing out that it was a legal personality separate, apart and distinct from its stockholders and, consequently, the covenant was not breached.[8] Despite what some say, not every corporation is evil.

Large corporations are complex organizations, or bureaucracies, that usually contain a hierarchy of authority, a division of labor, rationality in decision-making (finding the most efficient means to achieve a goal), and lots of written (formal) rules to regulate and control behavior. Although people frequently complain about bureaucratic "red tape," corporations are often the most efficient way to manage large numbers of people.

2. Entity Shielding

The second corporate element is entity shielding, which means the assets of the corporation are separate from the assets of the individual investors, owners or managers. A creditor seeking payment on a debt from a shareholder cannot force the corporation to pay the debt, as long as the two entities are separate. The reverse also is true: A shareholder normally cannot be forced to pay the debt of a corporation. (Unless they personally guaranteed the debt.)

Individual assets are to be used for individual purposes, and corporate assets for corporate purposes. As noted earlier though, when these assets become blended, the potential for veil-piercing increases.

3. Limited Liability

The third element is the doctrine of limited liability, which protects shareholders from liabilities created by the corporation. Voluntary creditors (such as lenders) and involuntary creditors (such as victims of corporate fraud schemes) can obtain compensation only from the corporation, not from its shareholders or owners. (Again, unless a personal guarantee is signed.)

In the case of a large corporation, the doctrine of limited liability is easy to justify, as shareholders, who often have little knowledge of the day-to-day operations of the company, should not be held culpable for the actions of managers who make bad financial decisions or engage in illegal or unethical behavior.

Limited liability is more difficult to justify, however, when it comes to small corporations, because the shareholder or owner is also managing the corporation. In fact, some people create LLCs with the intention of committing fraudulent actions. They often assume their personal assets are protected. But veil piercing is designed in part to provide a remedy for such illegal behaviors.

Types of Protective Entities

Statutory law varies from nation to nation and, in the United States, from state to state, but American entities come in five main types:

1. C Corporation

This form refers to businesses that, under federal law, are taxed separately from their owners. Most large businesses are C corporations, which have no limits on the number of shareholders or the types of shareholders (i.e., trusts or other entities.) In general, profits of C corporations are taxed once at the corporate level and then if the remaining funds are distributed to the shareholders, they are taxed again. Hence, the double taxation of the C corporation. Please note that salaries and bonuses are generally a pre-tax expense to the corporate employer.

2. S Corporation

This form of business passes corporate income, losses, deductions and credits through to their shareholders. This means income is taxed only at the shareholder level and not at the corporate level. In order to qualify as a S corporation, a business must have only one class of stock and no more than 100 shareholders, who must all be U.S. citizens or resident aliens.

3. Limited Liability Company (LLC)

An LLC blends elements of corporations and partnerships. Like the C and S corporation, it provides limited liability to its owners, and like an

Chapter Two

S corporation and a partnership, its profits are taxed as they pass through to the owners. Single-owner (or single-member) LLCs work the same way.

4. Limited Partnership (LP)

The limited partnership is a useful entity in certain circumstances, including estate planning. The general partner (GP) has absolute control and the limited partners are limited in their management activities. The GP, if consisting of individuals, is personally responsible for any claims. So, to encapsulate that unlimited GP liability into a limited liability entity, an LLC or corporation is formed to be the GP. As such, you need to form two entities for full LP protection.

5. Nonprofit Organization

Unlike a for-profit corporation, a nonprofit organization uses surplus revenues to achieve its beneficial goals rather than distributing them as profits. Employees who receive a salary from the nonprofit organization pay taxes on those earnings, of course.

I should note here that there are other forms of business, such as the sole proprietorship and general partnership. The doctrine of limited liability does not apply to the single owner of a sole proprietorship or to the general partner in a partnership. Many people start out this way because it is an easy and cheap way to operate. No extra filings with the state are needed. However, when they are sued, they learn the hard way that all of their personal assets are exposed to the claim.

What Is the Corporate Veil?

The word "veil" can be used as a noun or a verb. As a noun, as mentioned, it conjures up images of a piece of clothing worn by women to protect or conceal their faces. As a verb, it means to cover: "She veiled her face."

The use of the word "veil" is a fitting metaphor. As a legal concept, it separates the corporate form of organization from the personalities (and personal assets) of its shareholders or investors. But like most decorative veils, the corporate ones are not bullet proof. It isn't that hard to get behind them.

And yet, most large public corporations do stay protected. Lawsuits rarely ever pierce (or lift) their veils. First of all, most large companies have the resources to pay off any claim, so a piercing is not needed. Secondly, even if top management engages in illegal activities, passive shareholders who have no knowledge of such activities will not be held personally liable for management's actions. If the corporation goes under the investors lose their investment, but nothing else.

However, blanket protection does not apply to smaller corporations, usually those with less than 30 shareholders or investors. Single-member or small LLCs are the most vulnerable. Their veils are pierced more often than their larger counterparts. In fact, the percentage of piercings generally decreases as the size of the organization increases, perhaps because, as sociologists have discovered, the more owners or members in a business or organization, the more internal scrutiny there will be of illegal or unethical behavior. If you run a company by yourself you may have no one to check you, which is when having a good attorney and CPA on your team becomes important. Listen when they say: Don't do that.

Two Major Types of Piercings

Failing to fulfill the terms of a contract (or breach of contract) and acts of wrongdoing (or torts) are the two major types of piercings.

1. Contract Piercings.

A contract is an agreement, in writing or spoken, usually involving the exchange of money that is intended to be enforceable by law. Let's look at two examples. First, a mortgage loan. Rental property investors, through their LLC companies, borrow money from a lending institution and agree to pay the loan back over a specified amount of time. In almost all cases the lender will demand a personal guarantee from the borrowers. If they fail to pay the loan, they are said to be in default and the lending institution (the creditor) may sue both the LLC and the individual investors themselves.

With a personal guarantee (which says if the LLC doesn't pay the loan then I personally will) a creditor doesn't need to pierce the veil. They already have a claim against the individual borrower via the personal guarantee.

The second example is a standard business contract for services or goods. No personal guarantee is involved. When a vendor/creditor isn't paid by the company they can try to pierce through the entity and get paid by the individual owners. In this case, the entity's debts are paid only after the creditor pursues a claim against the individual owners. This is a hassle for the vendor/creditor.

As such, creditors have a much easier time collecting from owners who have personally guaranteed the obligation. However, as a business owner you want to avoid giving out personal guarantees if you can. You may have to provide a personal guarantee at the start. As your business gains its own credit rating you can rely on the business (and not yourself personally) for future guarantees. For more on establishing business credit, please see my book *Finance Your Own Business*.

2. Tort Piercings.

A tort is a wrongful act or an infringement of a right (other than under contract) leading to civil legal liability. An example is a person who is injured on a rental property. The injured person may file a lawsuit against your company and obtain a judgment from a court to pay damages and medical costs. A liability claim like this may cost millions of dollars, outstripping your LLC's insurance limits. As noted earlier, if the LLC has failed to follow state laws governing its form of organization, a court may pierce the veil and hold the individual owners personally liable for the claim. You don't want this to happen.

Generally, a contract piercing is relatively easy to avoid. Pay all of your debts and follow all laws. Don't let your business fall deep into debt and don't engage in fraudulent or illegal schemes.

They Can't Take My Assets, Can They?

A tort piercing is harder to avoid, because many tortious acts are unpredictable. Who can predict when someone might be injured at your business as a result of a fire or flood? (You'd be suspicious of anyone who could.) The best way to protect yourself from tort piercings is to (1) purchase adequate amounts of liability and casualty insurance, (2) keep your property safe, and (3) follow all rules governing your entity.

The history, logic and boundaries of the doctrine of limited liability provide an important foundation and are up next...

Chapter Three

How Did Limited Liability Evolve?

Imagine you're a successful merchant living in Europe before the 16th century. You have some gold you want to invest, but you're afraid to create a partnership to fund your cousin's blacksmith business. If your cousin's business goes under the creditors could come after your personal wealth. If your assets didn't cover the claims, you could be thrown into debtor's prison.

What are your options? Not many.

That's because the doctrine of limited liability for corporate forms of business had not yet evolved. Stock exchanges also didn't exist. They won't emerge for about another century.

But there was one option available to you: You could put your gold into an overseas trade expedition, which offered limited liability to investors. If the ship sank during a storm, you would only lose the amount you invested. Your business and personal assets were safe. The Royal Houses of Europe, in competition with each other, wanted exploration and trade, so exceptions were gradually made allowing for limited liability.

Although today the doctrine of limited liability is associated with private corporations, the concept emerged thousands of years ago. The only difference is that in those early centuries, limited liability was extended on a project by project basis and only rulers or the state had the power to grant the privilege. If you weren't royally connected and there was a business setback, well...off to debtor's prison with you. This, of course, was not a good way to advance economic activity. (Plus, how can you pay

Chapter Three

your debts back if you're in prison?) But, as is always true, certain powerful interests benefitted from the stagnation.

State Control of Limited Liability

From the 1400s to early 1800s, the granting of limited liability remained in the hands of the government in most nations.

In the 15th century, England granted limited liability to monastic communities and trade guilds (professional groups). Two centuries later the Crown granted the same to the East India Company and other trading groups. Prior to the 1850s, Parliament issued charters giving limited liability to companies building canals and railroads. Not until the mid-1850s was limited liability automatically extended to anyone who created a corporation.

Automatic Limited Liability

In 1811, New York became the first governmental entity in the world to offer limited liability to corporations without state approval. The practice spread quickly from state to state, in large part because many businesses moved to New York for the favorable laws. (To this day, people move from state to state for better laws.) By the mid-1800s, more than 20,000 corporations were operating in the United States. This greatly facilitated infrastructure development throughout America, as it was far more efficient to build roads, bridges, railroads, ports and manufacturing facilities through corporations than through partnerships or joint-stock companies. Mimicking the United States, other countries around the world automatically granted limited liability to anyone creating a corporation.

The law of limited liability remained fairly unchanged in the United States until 1977, when Wyoming enacted a law that allowed for the creation of limited liability companies (LLCs), including single-owner LLCs.

How Did Limited Liability Evolve?

The Limited Liability Company can be traced to a German entity known as the Gesellschaft mit beschranker Haftung (GmbH). Created in 1892 and combining limited liability with flow-through taxation, this entity soon found converts in a number of Latin American and European countries, including Portugal (1901); Panama (1917); Brazil (1919); France (1925); Chile (1929); Argentina (1932); Uruguay (1933); Mexico (1934); Belgium (1935); Switzerland (1936); Peru (1936); Columbia (1937); Costa Rica (1942); and Honduras (1950).

As United States businesses engaged in international commerce after World War II, many became exposed to the benefits of these foreign LLCs. Finally, Hamilton Brothers, an oil exploration firm that had used LLCs throughout Latin America, saw the benefits of the United States offering such an entity. They lobbied the Wyoming legislature (which involved buying everyone drinks at a Cheyenne bar across the street from the capitol) to enact LLC legislation and effective June 30, 1977, Wyoming became the first state to offer LLCs. Florida followed in 1982, and by 1994, all 50 states had enacted permitting legislation.

Why Limit Liability?

If you have already created an LLC or corporation, chances are you did so to protect your personal assets. That is sound reasoning.

But why would a nation or a state want to offer limited liability in the first place? What purpose, function or advantage does that doctrine provide for a government or for society as a whole?

Some legal theorists argue that limited liability is simply a consequence of corporate personhood — the separation of the individual from the business. Laws that allow for the chartering of corporations generally do not regard a corporation as an agent of its shareholders. Consequently, as the separation theory goes, shareholders should not be liable for the corporation's debts or wrongful actions.

However, what if there is only one owner, as is the case with single-member LLCs?

Chapter Three

Now it's not so easy to separate the individual from the legal entity, because the shareholder or owner is identical to the business entity.

Presumably no one understands this principle better than John Walkovszky, who was seriously injured when a taxi-cab owned by the Seon Cab Corporation in New York City struck him in 1962. Four years later Walkovszky filed a $500,000 personal injury lawsuit against William Carlton, who was sole owner of Seon Cab, which only carried $10,000 in insurance and had limited assets.[9] The complaint alleged that the cab driver was negligent and that Carlton's corporate business structure was an unlawful attempt "to defraud members of the general public," because it was deliberately undercapitalized to protect Carlton's personal and other business assets.

Seon Cab was one of nine other corporations that Carlton had created and owned, each of which operated only two taxi-cabs and carried the minimum automobile liability insurance required by law ($10,000 per cab). The plaintiff argued that Seon's corporate veil should be pierced, because these corporations, although seemingly independent of one another, are "operated ... as a single entity, unit and enterprise" with respect to financing repairs, supplies, garaging and employees.

A New York trial court granted Walkovszky's motion to pierce.

But the state appeals court overturned the ruling, rejecting the plaintiff's argument that Carlton "was conducting business in his individual capacity." The court pointed out that Carlton did not shuttle personal funds in and out of the company. Although the company had minimal assets, the court ruled that Carlton was not required to capitalize his company to meet the claims of Walkovzsky or any other tort victim. The court even acknowledged that Carlton deliberately created multiple companies to minimize his cost of liability insurance and his risk. But there is nothing wrong with that, the court stated, because that is why business people create corporations — to minimize risk. (At the time, by the way, most taxi-cab companies in New York City were similarly organized.)

The Walkovszky decision is often cited as one of the strongest arguments in defense of limited liability. Yet, it also has been strongly criticized for failing to provide a rationale justifying the conclusion that Carlton "was not conducting business in his individual capacity." In other words, the court was saying that Carlton's "personal ends" were separate from his "corporate ends," but how can that be when there is only one owner? As two legal scholars put it:

> As is true of most veil-piercing cases, Walkovszky involved a close corporation with a single dominant shareholder. In exercising that control, such a shareholder's decisions naturally are based on his own best interests. The corporation thus has no interests other than the interests of the dominant shareholder.[10]

Because of the difficulty of separating personal interests from corporate interests, at least when it comes to small LLCs, scholars and business people have searched for other grounds to justify the doctrine of limited liability. The most widely cited argument is that limited liability stimulates economic growth and that any dysfunctional effects produced by this process are of secondary concern.

The less one has to lose, the more likely one will take risks.

This proposition summarizes the logic behind the argument that limited liability stimulates economic growth. Business people will invest more if their risk is less.

But some see a downside to this argument.

If one reduces the investor's risk by enacting laws that grant them limited liability, does the risk to creditors and tort victims go up? If costs increase elsewhere, then does limited liability produce a social good, or is this simply a transfer of wealth from one group to another?

Proponents of limited liability counter that the answer to this issue is the free marketplace itself: Lenders will increase the costs of loans and tort victims will raise the amounts of damages in their lawsuits. So technically there is no transfer of wealth. But proving whether limited liability produces an economic benefit or social good involves a complex cost-benefit analysis. And until that is definitively known (if ever) the conventional wisdom, among both scholars and business people, is that limited liability produces a social good, because capitalism, with its job

Chapter Three

creation and higher living standards, would not have expanded so quickly in Europe and the United States had it not been for that doctrine.

And yet limited liability protection is only as good as your ability to keep it. To keep it, and to avoid a piercing of the veil, will be discussed next.

Chapter Four

How Can a Corporate Veil be Pierced?

You've been managing a single-member LLC for several years now, and things aren't going well. Your company is $200,000 in debt and your vendors won't extend any more credit.

You never knowingly engaged in fraudulent activity. You've always followed the laws on running your LLC. But now you and your company can't carry on. You have no alternative but to file for bankruptcy.

What is the likelihood your company's veil will be pierced?

Veil-piercing Standards

The answer to this question depends partly on the laws in the country or state in which your LLC was created, on the judge and/or jury assigned to your case, and on the nature of the complaint against your company. Rates of piercing across various jurisdictions can vary by as much as 70 percentage points.

Early in the 20th century, one U.S. District Court ruled that a piercing is justified when the "legal entity is used to defeat public convenience, justify wrong, protect fraud, or defend crime."[11] More recently, a California appeals court provided one of the most extensive lists of reasons for justifying a piercing. The defendant in that case was Oakland Meat and the long list is referred to here as the Oakland Meat list.[12] They are also referred to as corporate formalities which, as we've discussed, are part of the bull's-eye forever on your business:

Chapter Four

1. Commingling of funds and other assets, failing to segregate funds of the separate entities, and unauthorized diversion of corporate funds or assets to other than corporate uses;

2. The treatment by an individual of the assets of the corporation as his own;

3. The failure to obtain authority to issue stock or to subscribe to or issue the same;

4. The holding out by an individual that he is personally liable for the debts of the corporation;

5. The failure to maintain minutes or adequate corporate records, and the confusion of the records of the separate entities;

6. The identical equitable ownership in the two entities;

7. The identification of the equitable owners thereof with the domination and control of the two entities;

8. Identification of the directors and officers of the two entities in the responsible supervision and management;

9. Sole ownership of all of the stock in a corporation by one individual or the members of a family;

10. The use of the same office or business location;

11. The employment of the same employees and/or attorney;

12. The failure to adequately capitalize a corporation;

13. The total absence of corporate assets, and undercapitalization;

14. The use of a corporation as a mere shell, instrumentality or conduit for a single venture or the business of an individual or another corporation;

15. The concealment and misrepresentation of the identity of the responsible ownership, management and financial interest, or concealment of personal business activities;

How Can a Corporate Veil be Pierced?

16. The disregard of legal formalities and the failure to maintain arm's length relationships among related entities;

17. The use of the corporate entity to procure labor, services or merchandise for another person or entity;

18. The diversion stockholder or other person or entity, to the detriment of creditors, or the manipulation of assets and liabilities between entities so as to concentrate the assets in one and the liabilities in another;

19. The contracting with another with intent to avoid performance by use of a corporate entity as a shield against personal liability, or the use of a corporation as a subterfuge of illegal transactions; and

20. The formation and use of a corporation to transfer to it the existing liability of another person or entity.

Needless to say, the vast number of possible justifications for veil piercing has generated a fair amount of confusion among business owners and attorneys. The legal literature on the doctrine of limited liability is rife with complaints about vague statutory language and poor judicial rulings. Many complaints revolve around Numbers 12 and 13 on the list, both involving undercapitalization. How much money or assets are necessary to put into the company to eliminate this criterion for piercing? We will try and answer this question in Chapter 16, but...

Some states have laws requiring new businesses to have a minimum amount of assets (such as the $1,000 requirement in Texas), but these figures usually are so low they are meaningless. No court has ever set a standard, and the amount can vary wildly depending upon the industry and the business to be operated.

As well, Numbers 1, 2, 15, 18, 19 and 20 all relate to the transfers of money away from an entity responsible for payment, making collection difficult or impossible for a creditor. Emptying out a company or depriving it of funds after a judgment is rendered is a common strategy for many debtors.

Chapter Four

Such machinations are called 'fraudulent transfers' and it is now its own area of the law. A total of 43 states have adopted the Uniform Fraudulent Transfer Act to prevent such shenanigans. In Appendix A we cover the sub specialty of fraudulent transfer law for your benefit and use.

It is important to know that courts rarely grant veil piercings without some sort of fraud, negligence or plain old unfairness involved. And even then, not one but several of the Oakland Meat factors may need to be present. Unfortunately, consistency and clarity is not a feature of these cases and courts — even in the same state — will come up with inconsistent decisions. The situation is so complicated that some scholars have even called for an end to veil piercing altogether. But that is not going to happen. (I would not have written this book if it were.)

So let's look at the tests for piercing in a unique way so that they can be remembered. The courts generally use one of three different tests to determine whether to pierce the veil. The first is called the Two-Step (or Prong) Alter Ego Test and the second is the Instrumentality Test. Later in the book will discuss the third method: the Single Enterprise Theory.

1. The Alter Ego Test
When Superman Goes Bad

Alter ego refers to a second self or a suitable substitute. Clark Kent's alter ego is Superman. Dr. Jekyll's evil alter ego is Mr. Hyde.

In veil piercing alter ego refers to individuals and/or entities that are one in the same with the company to be pierced. Assessing whether Joe is one in the same with Joe's LLC is the first test, as cases ahead will further illustrate. If the answer is "No," they are not one in the same, then we go no further. There will be no piercing. But if the answer is "Yes," then the second test is put forth: Would the adherence to the doctrine of limited liability promote injustice or allow for a fraud or wrongful act?

The corporation has power, the ability to shield the individual's personal assets from risk. When the individual is found to be the alter ego of the corporation those corporate powers dissipate and we are left

How Can a Corporate Veil be Pierced?

with an individual without any power, and whose assets are now exposed. Consider this example:

A mild-mannered man dressed in business casual is seated at a rooftop bar. The bored bartender pours the man another drink. A second man walks in, sits down and orders a drink. After a few minutes the first man says: "Did you come here for the suspension patio?" The second man is unaware of it. The first man calmly walks off the deck and doesn't fall. He is suspended above the patio below. "You should try it." The second man says no thanks and orders another drink. "Suit yourself," says the first man as he — incredibly enough — walks about in thin air above the patio. He then returns to his seat and orders another drink.

After several more drinks, the second man decides he'll try the suspension patio. He walks off the deck and immediately falls, crashing onto the patio below, breaking his leg among numerous other injuries.

The bartender looks at the first man and says, "Superman. You're a jerk."

Of course, Superman, the Man of Steel and a most positive defender of truth and justice, would never engage in such a prank. But it serves as a twisted example of the alter ego doctrine.

Clark Kent, seated at the bar, is one in the same as Superman. The two are alter egos of each other. It is only when the more powerful of the two, Superman, misuses his powers that we have a problem.

When a corporation is one in the same with other individuals or entities, and those others then wrongfully misuse their alter ego corporation, the veil can be pierced. When the veil is pierced the corporate power of protection is gone. Like a judicial dose of kryptonite, everyone is now powerless and exposed.

Of note, the alter ego doctrine can be applied in cases where the parties are seemingly innocent.

Let's say Joe's LLC owes Mary Inc. $100,000. The LLC can't pay so a piercing claim is brought. Whether Joe and Joe's LLC are found to be one in the same can be decided by looking to Joe's handling of the corporate formalities.

Chapter Four

Joe didn't know he was supposed to keep corporate records and not commingle monies. He is innocent of intentionally ignoring the formalities. But he is held to the standard anyway. A good attorney can easily make the case that Joe is presumed to know the rules. If you want ongoing protection you follow the formalities. If you don't – whether you know them or not – you aren't entitled to any protection. Why should Mary Inc. be left holding the bag for $100,000 when Joe didn't know or follow the rules?

Let's look at the Seon Cab case again, where Mr. Walkovsky sued for his injuries. The court refused to declare that William Carlton's taxicab company operated as an alter ego. The court found no violations of corporate protections, no mixing of mortal with super hero. Carlton and his company were not identical and the power to protect remained in place. The veil didn't fail.

Alter ego tests often require a determination of whether a parent company has a distinct identity from a subsidiary company. This was the issue in *Fountain v. West Lumber Company*, [13] in which the plaintiff (Fountain) had a contract with C. R. Johnson and C. R. Johnson Lumber Company to perform work. The land and timber on which plaintiff was performing the work belonged to West Lumber Company, and when C.R. Johnson Lumber went into bankruptcy, West Lumber Company claimed all of the assets but left the debts with Johnson. Upholding the plaintiff's jury verdict against West Lumber, the Court held that: "if, notwithstanding the evidence relied on by the defendant..., the jury found that in fact the device of separate corporations was used in order to evade responsibility on the part of [West], Johnson being president and practically owner of all the stock in both companies, then the issue should be found in favor of the plaintiff." Fountain provided services and should be paid by someone.

Again, if the courts find no separation, the veil is not automatically pierced. In the Fountain case, the court found that Johnson was using his corporations to evade paying debts. In virtually all piercing cases, there are usually other grounds, such as fraud, to grant a piercing.

How Can a Corporate Veil be Pierced?

This is, then, the second part of the two-part alter ego test — a determination of whether adherence to the doctrine of limited liability would sanction a fraud or wrongful act or promote injustice. There is a considerable amount of variation from state to state and nation to nation when it comes to this part of the alter ego test. In California and Illinois, for example, the controlling language is "fraud and injustice." In Virginia, it's whether the company is "a device or sham used to disguise wrongs, obscure fraud, or conceal crime." But in virtually all alter ego cases, there is a wrong to right.

2. The Instrumentality Test
The Wizard of Oz is Bad

The second method for piercing the veil is with the Instrumentality Test. To succeed a plaintiff must show that:

1. The defendant (either an entity or person) dominated and controlled a corporation;
2. The defendant used that domination or control to perpetrate a fraud or wrong, and
3. The defendant's domination and control was the proximate cause of the wrong.

The instrument of power is best illustrated by the Wizard of Oz, who uses elaborate deceptions and tricks to project his authority. He controls and dominates the Emerald City apparatus for his own power.

To fully understand this piercing test it is useful to discuss certain interpretations of L. Frank Baum's classic children's story first published in 1900. Baum was a known trickster and, preferring questions to answers, never left any explanation behind. Into that vacuum many have inserted various explanations for a story that entertains on both a children's and a political level.

Chapter Four

The 1890's were a tumultuous time in America. Recession and industrial efficiencies left many workers unemployed. Brutal droughts and grasshopper invasions severely affected American farmers.

The very heated monetary question of gold versus silver affected all political discussions. The eastern monied interests favored a steady gold standard. Farmers and workers (politically known as Populists) wanted the free and unlimited coinage of silver, which allowed for a greater money supply and easier credit. Gold and silver are both measured in ounces. The abbreviation of ounces, or Oz, becomes the center of the story.

Baum's later interpreters assert that the Yellow Brick Road represents the gold standard. In the book, Dorothy, who is young, good and represents the American people, receives silver slippers after running down the Wicked Witch of the East. In the 1939 movie, which featured new Technicolor technologies, the slippers become ruby colored for better effect. (And the ruby slippers shine even brighter with Judy Garland in them.) The silver slippers Dorothy wears in the book represent the pro-silver movement arguing for easier money. Silver slippers on the Yellow Brick Road leading to Emerald City, the capital of greenback paper money, sets forth the conflict.

Along the way, Dorothy meets the Scarecrow, who represents the struggling American farmer, and the Tin Man, representing idled American workers. Some claim the Cowardly Lion is a metaphor for William Jennings Bryan, a Populist, pro-silver politician of the era who was cowardly for opposing the war with Spain in 1898. Others claim the Cowardly Lion represents the American people, once fierce and proud, but now cowardly in the face of new laws and regulations, as well as overbearing corporations and trusts that crush the spirit.

The four travel along the Yellow Brick Road towards Emerald City to seek help from the Wizard. The Scarecrow wants a brain, the Tin Man a heart and the Cowardly Lion some courage. Dorothy now realizes she just wants to go home.

Near the entrance to the city is a very large and colorfully resplendent poppy field. Opium, the drug of choice for the East India Company and others seeking docile populations, is derived from poppies. Dorothy and

How Can a Corporate Veil be Pierced?

the Lion, both living, breathing creatures, quickly become lethargic. The Scarecrow and Tin Man are not affected and cry for help. A snow arrives (with many metaphors later advanced) and the four are back on their way.

Emerald City, much like Panem in the Hunger Games series, represents the wealth and power of the government elites in contrast to the poorer hinterlands, where the roads are in disrepair. The Wizard is the supreme politician. He has the people believing he is wise and all powerful, but he won't do much other than effort to keep his power.

After delays, the four finally meet the Wizard, an apparition amid colored smoke and bursts of flames. Like most politicians, he won't grant any favors without a quid pro quo. As the dialog from the movie has it the Wizard states:

> "...Prove yourselves worthy by performing a very small task. Bring me the broomstick of the Witch of the West."
>
> "But," says the Tin Man, "if we do that we'll have to kill her to get it."
>
> "Bring me her broomstick and I'll grant your requests. Now go."
>
> "But," says the Lion, "what if she kills us first?"
>
> "I said go."

The Wizard can't lose. Either the Wicked Witch of the West kills the irritant that is Dorothy or somehow Dorothy kills one of his major rivals.

Surprisingly, the West Witch is 'liquidated' simply by being splashed with water (resulting in more allegorical speculation about the West and water.)

Back at Emerald City, with the requested broomstick, it is Toto's turn to shine. Throughout the movie Dorothy has conversations with her little dog. Many claim Toto represents the inner, intuitive self, that gut instinct never to be ignored.

Toto knows the Wizard is a fraud and pulls the curtain back to prove it. The old man, whose power has been sustained by elaborate deceptions, is just another manipulative politician. But he is also adroit. As played in the movie by popular character actor Frank Morgan, the Wizard turns on

Chapter Four

a dime to help out the four in a seemingly wise and genuine fashion, all the while also making plans for his own escape.

All ends well with Dorothy learning she has always had the power to return. The later interpretations argue this means the American people have always had the power to change course. But what about the Wizard? Did he know that before sending her on such a dangerous mission?

The Wonderful Wizard of Oz clearly entertains on two levels. First and foremost, it is a children's story. But it also serves as a symbolic representation of the Populist movement and the politics of Baum's times. One can only wonder what Baum and the Populists would think of our current era of easy credit and a ever expanding money supply most benefitting those who once wanted a stricter gold standard.

Now, back to the Instrumentality Test and piercing the veil. As mentioned, the Wizard dominated and controlled Emerald City, a true corporate apparatus, for his own purposes. The Wizard, an individual, was Emerald City. The Wizard used that power to perpetrate a wrong – sending Dorothy and company on a mission of death. Emerald City, the entity itself, did not need the broomstick. Only the Wizard did. And it was the Wizard's ability to dominate and control that led to the wrong – the murder of the Witch. The instrumentality test is applied in cases like the Wizard of Oz, where the instruments of corporate power are used by entities and individuals to perpetrate wrongful acts.

As mentioned, the Instrumentality Test involves three steps. In the first step, the plaintiff must prove that the defendant dominates the company or corporation so much that it has no separate mind, will or existence. Second, the plaintiff must demonstrate that the defendant used that control to commit a fraud or violate the plaintiff's rights. Third, the plaintiff must show that the control and breach of duty caused the plaintiff's injury. The third element distinguishes this test from the two-prong alter ego plus test, which implies but does not specifically mention the third condition.

Some legal scholars argue the Instrumentality Test "provides greater certainty" than the alter ego plus test. But the courts often are sloppy when applying it. In some cases, the courts grant a piercing even though they fail to apply the second and third conditions of the Instrumentality Test. Nevertheless, when it comes to piercing the veil, no matter which standard is used, it is important to remember that either Superman or the Wizard of Oz must have acted poorly. That is your key to the castle.

A third test, the Single Enterprise theory, where sister companies are mashed together as one new responsible entity (otherwise known as Sister Frankenstein) will be discussed in Chapter 19.

Proving Up a Piercing

If you ever find yourself in court it is important to know who does what. The plaintiff, the party who filed the complaint, has the burden of proving their claim. The defendant, in turn, can rebut the allegations with their own evidence in defense.

As a defendant, you aren't going to be held liable if the plaintiff is unable to produce the evidence. As well, most statutes also have a presumption against piercing, which means the law does not make it easy for plaintiffs to get at your personal assets. After all, if it were too easy, no one would want to create a corporation or an LLC, much less take a risk on anything.

Judicial systems in the United States and many other countries use three levels of standard of proof. The weakest level is a "preponderance of evidence", which means the plaintiff only has to show there is a greater than 50% chance that the claim is true. The strongest level is "beyond a shadow of a doubt", which is the standard used in criminal cases, when a juror delivers a verdict of guilt only when he or she is firmly convinced the defendant is guilty or when there is a real possibility the defendant is not guilty. In terms of quantifying this level of proof, legal scholars often put it at a 99% chance or higher that a crime has occurred and the defendant is responsible.

In-between these two extremes is a medium level of proof, which is called the "clear and convincing" evidence standard. This means the evidence is highly and substantially more likely to be true than untrue and the juror is convinced that the contention is highly probable. Putting

Chapter Four

a percentage on this proof is a bit more difficult than the other two standards, but a study of 170 federal judges found the average to be 75 percent.[14] Clear and convincing evidence is the standard normally used on disputes involving wills, fraud, and the withdrawing of life support.

Because there is a presumption against piercing the corporate veil, some legal scholars argue that the courts must use the clear and convincing evidence standard, not the less rigorous preponderance of evidence. In practice, though, courts vary, and in many instances a standard of proof is never debated or adopted. And even if one were adopted, some scholars believe many jurors have difficulty distinguishing between a preponderance of evidence versus clear and convincing evidence.

What is key are the facts of each case. A good attorney is going to present what happened in a way that a judge or jury feels that a wrong has been committed. That is the most important standard for the plaintiff's attorney: Was the wrong big enough to hold not just the corporation or LLC liable but the individual owners as well?

After a quick review we will consider specific cases dealing with this crucial element.

Chapter Five

A Quick Summary

The bull's-eye of personal risk for business claims is always on your business. A thin veil separates the corporate form of organization from the individual owners and their assets. The veil provides limited liability protection to the owners.

A court can order the veil to be pierced, or disregarded, when the owners engage in specific wrongful conduct. When a veil fails, the owners become personally responsible for the company's debt.

If the owners fail to uphold the separateness between the corporation and themselves then the court will not allow the veil to protect owners from corporate obligations. The veil will be pierced, and the plaintiff will have hit the bull's-eye.

Because in many cases the only way for a creditor to collect from a company is to pierce the corporate veil against the owners the issue is the most litigated area of corporate law.

Piercing cases are very fact specific and laws vary from state to state. There is no uniform body of law on piercing.

As a general rule, courts use three tests for piercing: The Alter Ego Test, the Instrumentality Test and the Single Enterprise Theory.

The Alter Ego Test (you remember, Superman) must overcome two hurdles. First, the court must find the entity to be as the owner's alter ego, meaning the owner and corporation are really one in the same. If the first hurdle is not met the court won't go on. If there is an alter ego finding then the second hurdle must be met. This requires a showing that piercing is appropriate to avoid unfairness or injustice.

The Instrumentality Test (like the Wizard of Oz example) involves three steps. First, the owner must control the corporation without separateness. Second, the owner used that control to commit a fraud. And third, that control and breach of duty must have caused harm to the creditor.

The Single Enterprise Theory (or our upcoming Sister Frankenstein) mashes sister companies together as one new responsible entity with personal liability imposed on the owners.

In almost all cases, no matter which test is used, the courts will not pierce the veil without a showing of some improper conduct.

Following corporate formalities from the outset is important. Even critics of the process realize that it is a slippery slope leading to personal liability dangers. As Jonathon Macey and Joshua Mitts wrote in the Cornell Law Review:

"[P]iercing the corporate veil for failing to observe corporate formalities such as holding directors' meetings or keeping minutes makes no sense. It is like imposing liability on a person because he did not wear a tie or keep a napkin in his lap while eating. . . .

"On the other hand, where the failure to keep records is so profound that one cannot utilize such records to determine which assets legitimately belong to the corporation and which legitimately belong to its shareholders, then piecing is appropriate to prevent the unfair and strategic abuse of creditors. . . ."[15]

Remember, too, that complete records are important to have when you want to sell your business. Too many business sales fall through for a lack of coherent documentation. Following the corporate formalities not only protects you from attack, it allows for a clean exit.

Many people will ask: Why not just use a land trust? There are no corporate formalities required with a land trust, right? The reason we don't use a land trust is the same reason we don't use a sole proprietorship or a general partnership. Neither of those forms have any rules to follow either. But all three of them—land trusts, sole proprietorships, and general partnerships—offer zero asset protection.

Wouldn't you rather follow some easy rules and be protected? Of course, its up to you. You're free to listen to land trust promoters who aren't focused on your protection once they've been paid.

How does following corporate formalities fit into the ESG movement?

ESG (which stands for: environmental, social and corporate governance) is an investing term for evaluating corporate behavior. Socially conscious investors now use ESG metrics to value a business and to determine whether or not to invest in a company.

Environmental factors relate to how a company operates as a steward of nature. Climate change and sustainability are among the key benchmark issues. Social criteria involves considering how a company interacts with suppliers, customers, employees and communities. Diversity and human rights are matters of importance. As to governance, investors will consider the ability of shareholders to vote on significant issues and the transparency of accounting methods before deploying their financial assets.

Levels of executive compensation and management structures featuring checks and balances are also of concern.

Accordingly, ESG is linked to a desire of many to only be associated with responsible investing.

By shunning bad actors and rewarding positive ones these investors believe market forces can be utilized towards beneficial outcomes. While following the required corporate formalities is certainly the most responsible way to run a company it doesn't necessarily rise to the level of the great social concerns posed by the ESG movement. Nevertheless, not following the formalities and having personal liability assessed is a very profound failure of corporate governance. No matter what the attitude or outlook of your investors, everyone will be united in their anger at you for allowing the veil to fail.

Now, let's review some key and illustrative cases...

Chapter Six

The Fredo Case – Breach of Fiduciary Duties

John Fredo was a retired engineer who had never invested in real estate before. He was to learn quite a lesson.[16]

Fredo had been friends with Bruno, a real estate professional, for many years. Fredo had loaned money to Bruno and had always been repaid on time. Bruno suggested that Fredo might want to consider investing in his limited partnership, which provided a 20% return.

Fredo was interested and learned of the 2536-38 South Walker Street property in Philadelphia, which was held by 2536-38 South Walker Street Associates, LP. The limited partnership was controlled by a general partner, Bruno Properties, Inc., (BPI) which owned one percent of the LP. The remaining 99% was owned by Bruno's two sons as limited partners. Conveniently, BPI was owned 100% by Bruno. As such, through the BPI general partner, Bruno had complete control of the LP.

Based on assurances that he would receive 10% of the LP's cashflow, Fredo invested $150,000 for a 10% limited partnership interest in the LP. A few months later, Fredo was convinced to put in even more money. For another $250,000 he would receive another 41% in the LP. Fredo mortgaged his house, borrowed money from his son and cashed in his IRA to come up with the money. It was by far the biggest investment he had ever made in his life.

The Amended Limited Partnership agreement now provided that Fredo would receive 51% of the cash flow, up from the 10% he had before. The investment was now structured as follows:

Chapter Six

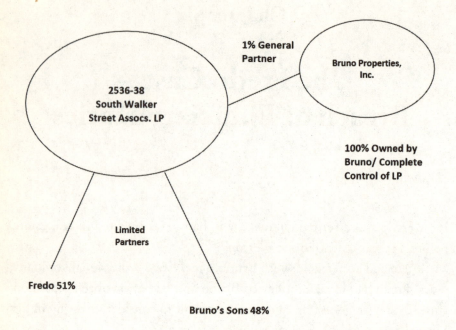

Upon reviewing tax returns, Fredo learned that Bruno had been paid a salary and developer fee by the LP. Bruno had never disclosed this to Fredo. Prior to Fredo's investment the LP had never paid Bruno any such fees. None of Bruno's other properties paid such fees. As well, the partnership didn't distribute any money to Fredo for three years. Bruno said he was having business troubles and, as a friend, Fredo let it slide.

But money and information were still not coming. Fredo hired an attorney to pursue the matter.

Bruno was having trouble at other properties. In order to provide collateral for debts he owed to contractors and lawyers on the other properties he granted deeds of trust against the South Walker Street property. The debts bore no relation to the South Walker Street property.

Over time, the LP collected over $2.5 million in rent from the tenants in the South Walker Street property. Fredo received no distributions. However, the trusts owned by Bruno's two sons, also limited partners, did receive distributions. As well, during this time, Bruno transferred $620,000 from the LP to his other troubled properties. Bruno later

The Fredo Case – Breach of Fiduciary Duties

claimed these were loans with "no paper trail." He also claimed that he did not know if the loans were ever paid back to the South Walker Street LP.

Fredo finally had enough and sued. At trial, Bruno maintained he had absolute authority through BPI as the general partner of the LP to direct the funds wherever he wanted.

The court disagreed, finding that BPI and Bruno, as general partner, owed a fiduciary duty to Fredo, the limited partner. By paying himself hundreds of thousands of dollars and by transferring hundreds of thousands of dollars more to entities Bruno controlled, Bruno became interchangeable with BPI, making Bruno personally liable for the breach.

A fiduciary duty is the highest requirement of trust there is, meaning Bruno could not put his interests above those of Fredo. There was plenty of evidence to find such a breach. As the court stated: "...whenever one in control of a corporation uses that control, or uses the corporate assets to further his or her own personal interests, the fiction of the separate corporate entity may be properly disregarded."

The court also found that by not keeping adequate and proper records of all the intercompany loan transactions that BPI, through Bruno, failed to observe the required corporate formalities.

Accordingly, the court found Bruno personally liable and ordered him to pay Fredo $642,000 on distributions he was entitled to along with $140,000 in interest.

As you can see, the facts of this case are pretty extreme. Setting aside legal niceties for a moment, Bruno screwed Fredo over. And that gets to the heart of fiduciary duties. You can't take money from people for an investment and then screw them over.

Duty: Something that one is required to do by legal obligation

You have certain duties when you run a company. As a corporate officer or director, an LLC manager or an LP general partner (hereinafter collectively referred to as an "officer") you must follow the legal rules and obligations that govern your situation. Your situation, as an officer in a position of trust, is one that calls for responsibility and integrity. And so

Chapter Six

know that the duties we discuss ahead arise from the law's preference for officers to do the right thing.

It is that simple. If every officer always acted with honor, we wouldn't need to articulate these duties. But since every officer—either through innocence or intention—doesn't so act, the following duties have evolved.

In a smaller company setting, where one or two people "are" the business, the distinctions to be reviewed are not as clear cut since everyone is doing everything. But even with everyone involved, the duties still remain. And as the company grows the duties take on even greater importance. Boundaries need to be in place within the organization or your growth can become unfocused, chaotic, challenged and headed for failure. When certain people act outside their mandate, when they act without authority, such activities can bring down the entire enterprise.

So, what follows is important for every company officer, manager and owner. As well, since the law requires it, it is important for you to know it.

General Overview

Our discussion of duties applies to all entities. For ease of use we will refer to corporations. But know that LLCs and LPs are equally as obligated to the rules of the company road.

From its birth until its dissolution, a corporation provides a set of unique relationships that imposes duties and responsibilities on the corporation's management. Following the shareholder's election of directors, and directors' appointment of officers in the organization meeting, the duties begin. As the corporation continues to develop and add managers and employees, there are an increasing number of questions about authority and duties. The relationship between shareholders, directors, officers and other employees may make corporate decision-making and actions more structured than in other business forms, such as sole proprietors and general partnerships. But this structure serves a purpose: Providing limited liability for all those involved.

Fiduciary Duties of Care & Loyalty

Generally, directors and officers are not personally liable for the obligations of the corporations that they serve. However, as we saw in the Fredo case, in cases of fraud or injustice, they can be held personally responsible. Corporate actors owe duties both to the corporation and its shareholders. These duties create the foundation for lawsuits brought by a corporation or its shareholders against directors or officers that act against the corporation's best interests. For example, unlike a piercing case, if an officer abuses his position and acts without authority, the corporation can bring a lawsuit against the officer for breach of fiduciary duties. In these cases, we are not piercing the veil that protects the owners. Instead, these cases take place ahead of the veil, within the corporation itself. Officers can be held personally responsible in such cases as well.

The foundation of all corporate fiduciary duties are the duties of care and loyalty. The following pages discuss the duties of care and loyalty in various contexts, but it is important to recognize that corporate officers and directors are not the only people that owe fiduciary duties. Managers and managing members in an LLC owe such duties. General partners owe fiduciary duties to the limited partners and to the limited partnership. Though shareholders do not generally owe duties to corporations, some states have held that majority shareholders owe such duties. Certain states, including Nevada, Wyoming and Delaware, have held that majority shareholders have fiduciary duties to the extent that they exert control over the corporation. This approach makes the exertion of power directly linked to fiduciary duties. As such, in any business context involving trust and control, fiduciary duties can arise.

Duty of Care

At its core, the duty of care requires corporate directors and officers to discharge their responsibilities with "due care." Their responsibilities include those for which they were specifically retained and those tangential to the office they serve. The definition of due care will vary based on the

Chapter Six

circumstances. The classic definition put forth by courts across the country provides that due care is that degree of care than an ordinarily prudent person in a like position would exercise under similar circumstances. The definition is intentionally vague. Each case is going to be different and dependent on facts and situations. Accordingly, each state has illustrated its understanding of due care through countless court cases. By reviewing those cases, one may begin to understand what is expected in each state.

A frequently litigated subject is the issuance of dividends. Many states, including Nevada, Wyoming and Delaware, provide by statute that the board of directors has the authority to issue dividends. The states' courts have afforded directors broad discretion in whether and to what extent to issue dividends. The duty of care only requires directors to avoid malfeasance or wrongful behavior in doing so.

In the context of merger or takeover attempts, directors and officers have a general duty to maximize shareholder wealth by seeking the highest possible price for shares of stock (though directors and officers who own stock and receive bonuses may have additional and conflicting duties in such a context). Courts may look to the method of determining the accepted price (e.g., independent analysis), the consideration given to the transaction (e.g., information from advisors, full and complete meetings, etc.), and the existence of any terms that substantially limit the directors' ability to obtain a fair price (e.g., terms that prevent an auction).

Directors also must accurately represent the transaction to shareholders. They cannot misrepresent the method of valuation, board approval, other options, or other terms of the transaction. Directors can protect themselves when presented with an opportunity to sell the company by hiring an investment banking firm to issue an opinion as to the fairness of the price offered.

Before delving into state court cases and special circumstances, however, it is important to note the corollary to the duty of care. The "business judgment rule" creates a presumption that fiduciaries are honest and well-meaning in performing their functions and that their decisions are informed and rationally undertaken. It presumes that directors do not breach their duty of care. It presumes that they use their business judgement, discussed ahead in Chapter 8, to reach a reasonable decision.

Duty of Loyalty

While the duty of care stems from an officer's performance of his or her duties, the duty of loyalty arises from the relationship between the corporation and its officers. As the Beach Boys' song suggests, you must be true to your company. Think of this duty in the same terms as an employee's covenant to not compete. The duty of loyalty prevents officers from doing anything that will negatively harm the corporation's business. While serving the company, officers cannot engage in active competition, solicit the corporation's customers or employees, or misuse confidential information or trade secrets. After the relationship with the corporation is terminated, former officers may cautiously engage in such competitive activities (unless they have signed a covenant not to complete).

Sitting on a corporate board is a position of control and power. The directors wield power that shareholders do not. The preferential and sometimes sycophantic treatment powerful directors receive from businessmen, bankers, and the like encourages certain individuals to be directors. How should this control be used?

Some directors will assume that they are entitled to some of that control for themselves, and that they are being generous when they provide any remaining benefits to shareholders. This is a distortion of corporate law (and yet another sense of entitlement issue within our society) leading to a potential for abuse. Duty of loyalty issues are not generally issues of control, but rather deal with the distinction between shareholder rights and the intentions (but not rights) of governing individuals.

Even greater distortions of entitlement arise when a corporation is dominated by a shareholder who also serves as a corporate officer and director. As mentioned above, majority shareholders may have the right to control, but they also have a fiduciary relation towards minority

Chapter Six

shareholders. In other words, even if you own 80% of the Company you still have a duty to the other 20% owners.

So when a shareholder/director votes as a shareholder, he may have the legal right to vote with a view of his own benefits and represent himself only. But when a shareholder/director votes as a director, he represents all the shareholders as a trustee and cannot use his office as a director for personal benefit at the expense of the shareholders. Before acting to the detriment of the minority, the majority shareholder must make full disclosure to allow the minority to protect itself in whatever way possible.

Controlling shareholders are often imposed with the same duties as the board of directors: Courts realize that the board may be a dummy for the controlling shareholder. While controlling your own money is fine, controlling others' money creates a duty of loyalty.

A frequent problem arises in larger settings when board members also sit on other corporate boards. Interlocking directors (where one or more people sit on two boards and are thus interlocked) can create issues if such directors have financial interests in both corporations. Interlocking control and ownership can be a factor in piercing the veil.

As well, interlocking directors may present control issues for the corporation. To sanitize transactions and decisions involving interlocking directors, the corporation may seek ratification from shareholders. This may be problematic in many cases, because the shareholders may not be willing to ratify the transaction (and perhaps with good reason). Nevertheless, failing to obtain ratification may lead to claims for a breach of the duty of loyalty.

The duty of loyalty is multifaceted. It arises in cases involving executive compensation, trading on insider information, selling out, and most importantly, taking away corporate opportunities.

Shareholders can sue the company on such claims.

Let's explore corporate opportunities and shareholder derivative suits a bit more...

Chapter Seven

Corporate Opportunities
Entitled Officers – Angry Shareholders

The simplest case involving a breach of the duty of loyalty is where a corporate executive expropriates for themself a business opportunity that rightfully belongs to the corporation. For example, assume that a company distributes window shades but a key executive takes the exclusive distributorship rights for a new type of awning. The corporation should have obtained the distributorship. It is in their core business. The duty of loyalty requires officers and directors to apprise the corporation (or LLC or LP) of "corporate opportunities." The corporation gets to decide if it wants it or not. If the company doesn't move forward then the executive may be free to pursue it, or not. The decision may be at the company's discretion.

A corporate opportunity is any investment, purchase, lease or any other opportunity that is in the line of the corporation's business, and is of practical advantage to the corporation. If an officer or director embraces such opportunity by taking it as their own, they may violate their duty of loyalty, especially if by doing so their self-interest will be brought into conflict with the corporation's interests. Will the officer be loyal to the company or their own business? The conflict is clear.

During their time in office, officers will likely discover business opportunities for the corporation. The officer may also have personal business opportunities that are somehow related to the corporation's business. For example, if the officer is an inventor who focuses on telecommunications products, they will likely be interested in all such

Chapter Seven

business opportunities. The corporation may be able to pursue some opportunities the officer discovers for the corporation, others it will not. If the corporation turns down one opportunity is the officer then able to pursue it?

Delaware courts have established a test for corporate opportunities. If an officer's self-interest comes into conflict with the corporation's interest, the duty of loyalty can be breached. The law will not permit an officer to pursue opportunities (1) that the corporation is financially able to undertake, (2) that is in the line of the corporation's business, and (3) that is of practical advantage to the corporation. On the other hand, if the corporation is not financially able to embrace the opportunity, has no interest in the opportunity, and the officer does not diminish their duties to the corporation by exploiting the opportunity, then the person may be allowed to pursue the opportunity.

Evidence that the opportunity was presented directly to the individual, and then not shared with the corporation, may be used to show that the corporate opportunity rules were not followed. In most states, the simplest way to avoid a problem is to present the opportunity to the corporation and allow it the chance to pursue or reject it. If the corporation cannot or will not take advantage of the opportunity, the employee, officer, or director may be free to pursue the opportunity. Though formal rejection by the board is not strictly necessary, it is safer for the whole board to reject a corporate opportunity. The decision shouldn't be based on individual board member's opinions. There must be a presentation of the opportunity in some form. After the corporation has rejected the opportunity, and before pursuing the opportunity, the employee, officer, or director should unambiguously disclose that the corporation refused to pursue the opportunity and ensure that there is an explanation for the refusal.

Resignation before completion of the questionable activity may not constitute a defense to liability arising from a corporate opportunity. Courts have found liability even where officers and directors resigned before the completion of the transaction. Although there are no certain guidelines for determining which opportunities belong to the corporation, controversy and liability may be avoided if officers use rigorous caution regarding corporate opportunities. If an issue arises, consult with your attorney.

Rigorous caution was not found in the eBay case.[17] The corporate opportunity was receiving the lucrative right to buy shares in other company's IPO offerings. Should those rights go to the individual board members or the company itself? The eBay board of directors vigorously claimed that the rights were theirs, as individuals. The company didn't earn them. Instead, it was the brilliance of the board that earned the rights. The directors also claimed that everyone in Silicon Valley did 'it' this way. But the Delaware Court of Chancery didn't care who did 'it' this way, since 'it' was wrong.

The 'it' was spinning, whereby an investment banker allocates initial public offering shares in other companies to favored insiders, like eBay's board members. eBay's shareholders did not like 'it' one bit and sued. As the Delaware Court stated:

> "In effect, the plaintiff shareholders allege that Goldman Sachs bribed certain eBay insiders, using the currency of highly profitable investment opportunities – opportunities that should have been offered to, or provided for the benefit of, eBay rather than the favored insiders. Plaintiffs accuse Goldman Sachs of aiding and abetting the corporate insider's breach of their fiduciary duty of loyalty to eBay."

The court plainly noted that eBay, the world's first billion-dollar garage sale platform, invested for its own account with all its pennies in profits from selling tchatkas. It's 1999 10k public report showed eBay had more than $550 million invested in equity and debt securities. If Goldman was going to spin out lucrative stock allocations they should have gone to eBay itself, an actively investing company, and not to the insiders usurping a corporate opportunity. The shareholders, who didn't benefit from Goldman's largesse, had solid arguments. As the court stated:

> "This was not an instance where a broker offered advice to a director about an investment in a marketable security. The conduct

Chapter Seven

challenged here involved a large investment bank that regularly did business with a company steering highly lucrative IPO allocations to select insider directors and officers at that company, allegedly both to reward them for past business and to induce them to direct future business to that investment bank. This is a far cry from the defendants' characterization of the conduct in question as merely "a broker's investment recommendations" to a wealthy client.

Nor can one seriously argue that this conduct did not place the insider defendants in a position of conflict with their duties to the corporation. One can realistically characterize these IPO allocations as a form of commercial discount or rebate for past or future investment banking services. Viewed pragmatically, it is easy to understand how steering such commercial rebates to certain insider directors places those directors in an obvious conflict between their self-interest and the corporation's interest. It is noteworthy, too, that the Securities and Exchange Commission has taken the position that "spinning" practices violate the obligations of broker-dealers under the "Free-riding and Withholding Interpretation" rules. As the SEC has explained, "the purpose of the interpretation is to protect the integrity of the public offering system by ensuring that members make a bona fide public distribution of "hot issue" securities and do not withhold such securities for their own benefit or use the securities to reward other persons who are in a position to direct future business to the member."

But unlike the eBay case, not all opportunities are suspect.[18] However, some bankruptcy trustees like to think so (which provides them with their own opportunities.)

Babson Electronics did business in Medford, Massachusetts and paid $2,800 a month in rent. Marty Babson, the sole owner of the company, felt he could do better in New Hampshire and started looking for a property he could personally buy and then rent to his company. Marty knew that having his business use pre-tax dollars, the expense of rent,

Corporate Opportunities

to pay the mortgage on a building he owned was an excellent business strategy. Many of his business contemporaries had done the same, to their great benefit upon retirement when they sold the business and kept the income generating building.

In August 1981 Marty found his New Hampshire property. He put $5,000 down with personal funds and became personally responsible for an assumed mortgage on the property of $64,000. Marty had previously loaned Babson $21,000 and using a cashier's check he drew the money out of the company with himself as the payee. He then endorsed the check over to the seller. The transaction closed and Marty leased the property to his company at a $900 savings over what he had paid in Massachusetts. Marty personally paid for all taxes, utilities and insurance on the property.

Two years later Babson Electronics, Inc. ran into trouble and filed for a Chapter 7 liquidation bankruptcy. Trustee Dick Nanny was assigned to the case and promptly sued for imposition of a constructive trust, claiming Marty had used corporate funds to buy and maintain the New Hampshire property.

A constructive trust is imposed by court order when one party obtains a legal property right through wrongful manipulation, including breaching a fiduciary duty. The trust is not explicitly formed in a writing but is rather implied by conduct of the parties and thus created by the court to right a wrong. Trustee Dick Nanny claimed Marty had breached a corporate opportunity by buying the property in his name, and using corporate funds to do it. The corporate opportunity, Nanny argued, stood with the company, not its owner. The bankruptcy court and district court agreed with Nanny and the constructive trust they imposed took the property from Marty for the benefit of the bankrupt company (and the trustee fees being generated by Dick Nanny.)

The district court saw through it:

> "We must keep in mind that Marty was the sole shareholder, director and president of Babson. Because the corporate opportunity doctrine is a rule of disclosure, application of the rule is inapposite where an action taken by Marty necessarily involves

Chapter Seven

the knowledge and assent of the corporation. Marty cannot be accused of defrauding or concealing information from himself in his role as sole corporate director...The ownership of all the stock and the absolute control of the affairs of a corporation do not make that corporation and the individual owner identical, in the absence of a fraudulent purpose in the organization of the corporation... But, absent some element of defrauding, Marty was not obliged, in every action he took to prefer the corporation's interests to his own. No one could operate a corporation solely on such a basis... We find that under any theory of liability for breach of fiduciary duty, Marty's behavior was entirely proper for the sole shareholder of a close corporation. The law is clear that the rights of creditors are involved only where there has been prejudice to creditors, and prejudice arises where the transaction is a fraudulent conveyance or one which led to corporate insolvency...We find no prejudice to creditors in this case. Babson was solvent at the time of the move to New Hampshire."

The district court lifted the constructive trust. Marty got his property, which was always rightfully his through a legitimate leasing strategy, away from a fee generating bankruptcy trustee.

Sometimes the corporate opportunity doctrine must be questioned in those who sue over corporate opportunities, as the bankruptcy trustee did in this case.

There are two more questions to ask and answer regarding corporate opportunities.

First: Can you pierce the veil over a corporate opportunity? Yes. If the corporation, in order to avoid taking in money so as to not pay a creditor, gives the opportunity to an owner instead, a claim of personal liability could arise. Breaching a fiduciary duty to prejudice known creditors will not end well in most cases. You may find yourself personally liable.

Second: Can shareholders sue the company for the failing of its officers?

Corporate Opportunities

That is exactly what happened in eBay case. Shareholders sued the corporation–for the benefit of the corporation. This may sound odd, and kind of like the war time strategy of destroying a city to protect it. But such cases, known as shareholder derivative suits, since they are derived from the shareholder's ultimate ownership of the company, do make sense. In these legal actions, shareholders who own the entity bring a lawsuit on the corporation's behalf to enforce the corporation's rights against officers and directors.

Before a shareholder may pursue such a claim, however, they must present the claim to the corporation and provide the corporation an opportunity to pursue its own claim. The claim basically tells the corporation that if they don't sue, the shareholders will. A corporation may then create a litigation committee to evaluate the merits of the shareholder's claim and make an impartial decision regarding whether to pursue litigation. If a shareholder's derivative suit challenges the litigation committee's decision not to pursue legal action against a director, the business judgment rule (discussed next) will be applied to the committee's decision, unless bad faith is demonstrated.

Of course, as a practical matter, not many corporations are willing (or can even be nudged) to sue their own officers and directors. This is why the shareholder derivative suit was allowed in the first place, as a remedy to keep officers and directors honest. Over the years many of these types of suits have been successful.

For directors to settle a shareholder derivative suit, the settlement must be fair and reasonable.

Plaintiff shareholders may show that a settlement is unreasonable by showing that the directors knew or should have known that violations of the law were occurring and that such failure proximately resulted in losses to shareholder detriment. Yet only a sustained or systematic failure of the board to exercise oversight will establish the lack of good faith that is a necessary condition to liability. A settlement may be considered fair and reasonable if it remedies the procedural problems within the corporation that had led to the underlying litigation.

Chapter Seven

The duty of care depends not only on the nature of the transaction, but also upon the nature of the corporation itself. For example, while directors generally do not owe duties to creditors unless the corporation is insolvent, directors of banks and insurance companies owe creditors increased duties because they hold the funds of others in trust. Think of a bank. Your deposit doesn't belong to the directors. Accordingly, such directors are under a duty to read financial statements, detect a misappropriation of the funds, and protect the clients against other directors' illegal conduct. While the nature of the duty depends upon the company's activities in general, a director should at least acquire a rudimentary understanding of the corporation's business. (Remember this if you are asked to join a Board of Directors.)

As well, directors are under a continuing obligation to keep informed about the corporation's activities. If a director discovers an illegal course of action, he or she must object and, if the corporation does not correct the conduct, they should resign or take reasonable means to prevent illegal conduct by co-directors. All of which can be problematic, so be sure you know what you are getting into and consult your attorney on any issues.

States apply differing standards to enforce directors' and officers' duty of care. For example, while most states are willing to hold directors and officers personally liable for a breach of their fiduciary duties, Nevada is more resistant to do so. A Nevada statute (discussed next) provides that Nevada courts should not hold directors or officers personally liable unless they committed an intentional breach of their fiduciary duties, engaged in fraud, or knowingly violated the law. Instead of simply requiring evidence of a breach, Nevada law appears to require proof that the offender knew that he or she was doing wrong, an element typically reserved for criminal offenses. This standard is higher than that applied by other states. This, of course, provides another good reason to use Nevada corporations. But know that in the Fredo case, even Bruno would be held personally liable in Nevada.

Now let's check your business judgment...

Chapter Eight

Bull's–eye on Business Judgment

In the law it is important to appreciate the concept of precedent. While legislatures pass laws, courts have to interpret them and flesh them out. You don't want courts applying inconsistent standards and rulings everywhere. Citizens, for the most part, actually try and follow the law. They need help from the courts to do so. Courts rely on precedent, those previous decisions of other courts, to provide clarity and cohesion to their current decisions. Precedent, then, provides a stable foundation of understanding which can be modified, if needed, as you continue to build.

To continue the construction analogy, sometimes the architect notices a flaw that must be corrected. It may be a tweak or a complete rebuild but their obligation is to provide a cohesive and solid structure. Judges have the same obligation. If a decision is slightly misinterpreted later or completely gets away from their original intent, judges have the power to change and clarify for the good of the framework. New precedent is allowed. When the laws of several states are inconsistent with each other, the U.S. Supreme Court, as the final court for decisions, may step in and clarify any previous precedent. Allowing some flexibility for the law to evolve is, all in all, beneficial.

That is the scenario in our next case involving the business judgment rule. Before discussing the Pike case[19] an understanding of the business judgment rule is in order.

Courts apply the business judgment rule when considering breaches of the duty of care. Under this rule, courts presume that the business

Chapter Eight

decision was proper, regardless of the result, and that the decision was made in good faith and with the honest belief that the action taken was in the corporation's best interests. The presumption may be rebutted in most states if the plaintiff shows that the decision was tainted by fraud, a conflict of interest, or self-dealing.

The business judgment rule also encourages businesses to take risks by insulating officers and directors from liability. The intent is to limit judicial meddling and second guessing in business decisions. Our economy and society do not improve when opportunity leads to jeopardy. Uncertainties are not useful here. Profit corresponds to risk. It is in the shareholders' (as well as the nation's) best interest that the law does not lead to overly cautious corporate decision making. The business judgment rule is uniquely prudent in allowing risk.

The business judgment rule also encourages officers and directors to serve without fear of being judged in hindsight. A corporate officer who makes a mistake in judgment as to economic conditions, consumer tastes or production line efficiency will rarely, if ever, be found liable for damages suffered by the corporation. Not all lapses of judgment constitute a breach of the duty of care. Simple mistakes and poor business judgment generally will not create liability. If it did, we'd all work for the government.

To ensure that the business judgment rule is applied, directors and officers (especially in larger corporate settings) should create and maintain corporate procedures. Courts often focus on the procedure involved in decision making, not the merit of the decision. Directors are generally immune from liability if they in good faith rely upon the opinion of counsel, written reports setting forth the financial data prepared by a CPA, or upon financial statements, books of account, or reports of the corporation presented by the president or financial officer. Evidence of collecting information, using expert advisors (especially outside advisors), deliberation, and documentation may prevent malfeasance and may protect directors and officers from liability. The presence and role of outside independent directors (those not working within the company) in decisions may determine whether a court will permit an otherwise questionable decision. Outside directors are privy to less information than

Bull's-eye on Business Judgment

insiders regarding the daily operations of the business, but are under an equal duty to act in the corporation's best interests.

Outsiders have a duty to seek information regarding the business's activity. (Remember that if you are an outside director).

Courts have generally held that all directors have a duty to reasonably ensure that adequate corporate information and reporting systems exist. Corporate formalities such as the preparation and presentation of annual minutes must be properly handled.

While the business judgment rule generally protects officers and directors from courts second- guessing their business decisions, it does not provide an absolute protection. Any action tainted by fraud can be invalidated. Board members can be liable for personally benefitting from a conflict of interest. If decisions reflect gross negligence or recklessness, in some states the business judgment rule will not protect the officer or director. (Choice of state law, as discussed in Chapter 11, becomes important here).

The business judgment rule does not apply in cases where the corporate decision lacks a business purpose or is so egregious as to amount to a no-win decision. Additionally, courts may hold officers and directors liable for making decisions without adequately investigating other solutions or adequately supervising decision makers. That said, good-faith board decisions will be protected from second guessing. Only a neglect of duties (nonfeasance), and not misjudgment, is actionable. Nevertheless, the standards courts apply depend on the court and the circumstances of each case.

The standards before the Nevada Supreme Court for Nevada's fiduciary duty of care and the business judgment rule were at issue in Pike.

CTJ Risk Retention, Inc. insured long term health care facilities across the country and ran into trouble. In 2012, the Nevada Division of Insurance filed a receivership action against CTJ. When companies fail (especially in the fields of insurance and finance) the state can appoint a receiver, a person or organization who 'receives' what's left of the company and tries to sort everything out. In this case the receiver was Nevada's Commissioner of Insurance. After reviewing it all the receiver sought a

Chapter Eight

court order to liquidate and wind up CTJ. The court order also gave the Insurance Commissioner, as some government agencies like to do, the power to go after CTJ's directors (collectively "Pike") as individuals for the wreckage they caused.

The Commissioner filed a complaint against Pike for breaching the fiduciary duty of care by engaging in gross negligence. It was alleged that Pike was grossly negligent for not knowing of CTJ's precarious financial status and failing to take corrective action. The Commissioner sought to hold Pike personally responsible for the failure of an insurance company, which sent a chill throughout the insurance community. Who'd ever serve as a company director with that risk hanging over them?

Pike's attorney's response in defense was: "Hold on here. You can't do that. The Nevada Code says you can't hold Pike personally responsible for this." The code section they correctly put forth is *NRS 78.138* (which is found in full in Appendix B and offers another benefit to incorporating in Nevada). The specific part of the code, *NRS 78.138 (7)*, states that directors and officers aren't individually liable to the corporation, shareholders or creditors for any damages unless:

(1) The director's or officer's act or failure to act constituted a breach of his or her fiduciary duties as a director or officer; and

(2) Such breach involved intentional misconduct, fraud or a knowing violation of the law.

The Insurance Commissioner fought back, relying on the *Shoen* case, which had been decided by the Nevada Supreme Court in 2006. The Commissioner argued that *Shoen* allowed claims of gross negligence to proceed against individual directors.

How would the Court rule here?

Precedent would argue for the *Shoen* case and personal liability. But the code sought to protect individuals. And codes can trump case law. In fact, bad case law can be remedied by new code sections passed by federal and state legislatures. But some courts will try and thread the needle with 'subtly distinct' and 'nuanced' interpolations between case law and code.

Bull's—eye on Business Judgment

And yet splitting the baby, while always bad for the baby, isn't much better in the law.

The Nevada Supreme Court went for clarity:

> This case requires us to consider whether a corporate director or officer may be held individually liable for breaching his or her fiduciary duty of care through gross negligence. Statutorily, a director or officer is not individually liable for harm resulting from official actions unless the director or officer engages in "intentional misconduct, fraud or a knowing violation of law." *NRS 78.138(7) (a)-(b). In Shoen v. SAC Holding Corp., 122 Nev. 621, 640, 137 P.3d 1171, 1184 (2006),* however, we stated that "with regard to the duty of care, the business judgment rule does not protect the gross negligence of uninformed directors and officers." As a result, some courts, including the district court here, have allowed claims against individual directors and officers to proceed based only on allegations of gross negligence.
>
> We now clarify that, based on the plain text of the statute, *NRS 78.138(7)* applies to all claims of individual liability against directors and officers, precluding the imposition of liability for grossly negligent breaches of fiduciary duties. We further conclude that the gross negligence-based allegations in the operative complaint below fail to state an actionable claim under *NRS 78.138.*

In two succinct paragraphs the Court cleared up an issue of great concern. Unless a director acts with knowing bad intentions, their decisions will not render them personally responsible. The Court both supported the Nevada legislature's specific, clearly worded statutory intent to protect officers and directors and corrected a gap in their own case law framework. Lawyers appreciate straight up judges.

Nevada took further steps to strengthen business judgement rule protections in the Guzman case.[20] To hold a director responsible for corporate decisions, a party must "**both** rebut the business judgement rule's presumption of good faith **and** show a breach of fiduciary duty

65

Chapter Eight

involving intentional misconduct, fraud, or a knowing violation of the law." The mere allegation that a director was an interested party was not enough to shift the burden onto the director to show that the transaction was fair.

In contrast, Delaware courts are much more likely to allow a fairness review, to the detriment of corporate officers and directors. A number of legal commentators have noticed that for this reason alone, Nevada may be the superior state for LLC and corporate formation. (I know, I've mentioned it several times.)

The business judgment rule does have its limits. Officers and directors who engage in self- dealing to the detriment of the corporation, shareholders and creditors will not always be protected, as our next case reveals.

Dock Printing, Inc.[21] took a bad turn and entered into bankruptcy. As in a receivership where a receiver is appointed by a court to come in and call the shots, in bankruptcy a trustee is designated to review the situation and either reorganize or wind up the company. They have powers independent from the officers and directors and, if appropriate, a trustee, on behalf of the company, can bring suit against the officers and directors.

While independent from the facts of Dock, it is important to know that within our legal system receivers and trustees have significant economic incentives that must be clearly understood. Receivers and trustees get paid for their time. The more time they put in the more they get paid. Receivers and trustees, who don't have to be attorneys, can bring in their attorney friends to represent them. When the receiver or trustee and their attorneys bring suit against officers, directors or anyone else, everyone on their side gets paid. If a settlement is reached it's usually only after the tank is near empty after the payment of 'services' they rendered. In bankruptcy most people envision the dead carcass of a company. And yet in these cases certain professionals still manage to come away very well fed. You get the analogy.

A key business strategy should always be to keep any court appointed anybody out of your company. Business people universally rue the day that a receiver or trustee entered their world. They liken it to a Twilight Zone of

Bull's-eye on Business Judgment

beyond normal. Try to avoid such a loss of control. Try at all costs to work things out. Check your pride. Make concessions. Find common ground. Even if you are down, don't be a jerk. Work to get through it knowing you are far better off maintaining whatever control you have than turning it over to someone with a court sanction who can legally squander your assets.

In Dock Printing, the North Carolina bankruptcy trustee sued the officers and directors (collectively "Defendants") for selling all of Dock's assets to a third party at a ridiculously low price, to the detriment of Dock's other creditors.

The general rule in North Carolina is that corporate directors don't owe a fiduciary duty to the corporation's creditors. However, when a corporation is winding up or dissolving the directors DO owe a fiduciary duty to the creditors. Take note of that wrinkle.

The Dock Bankruptcy Trustee maintained that the sale was for grossly inadequate consideration, and was undertaken by the Defendants to satisfy an unsecured bank debt that they had personally guaranteed. The Trustee maintained that the Defendants personally had benefitted from this "fire sale" (by extinguishing their own personal guarantees to the bank) to the detriment of the debtor and its creditors, and in so doing breached fiduciary duties owed by themselves to both Dock and its creditors. The Trustee sought recovery of damages from the individual directors.

The Defendants countered that their decision to terminate Dock's business operations by selling its assets was in the best interests of the company, given that there were no other offers or viable alternatives.

The Defendants further argued that Dock's board of directors reluctantly made the decision to sell due to Dock's default on a line of credit to its bank, the ensuing demand by the bank for turnover of collateral, and a lack of cash flow by which to keep the company operating. Finally, the Defendants asserted that, until the eve of the closing, the Board believed the bank held a valid and perfected secured lien on all of Dock's assets. By the time it learned otherwise, the Board was committed to the sale and

Chapter Eight

could not avert course. The Defendants claimed they breached no duties under the circumstances.

By transferring assets without obtaining reasonably equivalent value for them, as claimed by the Trustee, when the assets could have otherwise been available to satisfy creditors' claims, the Bankruptcy Court logically focused on the business judgment rule. The Court noted that North Carolina's business judgment rule generally protected a corporate director from liability for actions. However, the Court pointed out that the business judgment rule did not apply if the corporate directors had engaged in self-dealing, fraud, or other unconscionable conduct.

As such, the Court found that the Trustee had alleged specific facts to overcome the presumption of the business judgment rule. The Court reasoned that the Trustee had alleged self-dealing on the part of the Defendants in that they were able to get their personal guaranties released or indemnified as part of the transaction with the buyer of Dock's assets, a transaction granting the Defendants a direct financial benefit. The case went forward.

Self-dealing can get interesting, as illustrated in our next case...

Chapter Nine

The Wallop Case – Self Dealing?

Malcolm Wallop was the U.S. Senator from Wyoming from 1977 to 1995. He came from a family of titled English aristocrats. There were many British peers in the West after the Civil War. Oliver Wallop, Malcolm's grandfather, immigrated to Wyoming in the late 19th century to pursue cattle ranching. When his older brother died young, Oliver inherited the Earldom of Portsmouth. Interestingly, and perhaps not surprisingly, Oliver is the only person to serve in both the Wyoming House of Representatives and the British House of Lords. The aristocratic ties ran deep. Queen Elizabeth stayed at Malcolm Wallop's Canyon Ranch in Big Horn, Wyoming during her 1984 visit to the United States.

Malcolm's nephew is George Herbert, the 8th Earl of Carnarvon, whose family home is Highclere Castle, the location used for the filming of Downton Abbey.

Throughout history titled landowners have fought wars and duels, committed violence and mayhem, and engaged in poisonings, patricide, matricide, convenient 'suicide' and other nefarious deeds to avenge and gain control of real estate. In America these disputes go to court.

Malcolm and his third wife, French, set up an estate plan in 1992 for the Canyon Ranch. The Wallop Family Limited Partnership (WFLP) owned and operated the Canyon Ranch.

They also formed Wallop Canyon Ranch LLC (WCR), a Wyoming limited liability company, to serve as the general partner (or GP) of WFLP. WCR was owned 50/50 by Malcolm and French.

Chapter Nine

Every limited partnership (LP) must have, by definition, at least two partners. One is a limited partner whose exposure in the investment is limited to the amount of money invested. Meaning if they invested $5,000, they can only lose $5,000 and not be held personally liable for any further monies.

They are also limited in their role and cannot assert a right to manage the business. The general partner, the required second partner, has all the management authority. With that comes liability for all actions within the LP. To minimize that unlimited liability, an LLC or corporation is set up to serve as the general partner. In this way the general partner liability is encapsulated into a limited liability entity.

The initial partners of WFLP were Malcolm with 49% and French with 49%. WCR, the general partner (and as is standard in most limited partnership arrangements) owned 2% of WFLP.

The LP is a good estate planning vehicle for transferring ownership to the younger generation.

The limited partners can gift their interests to the kids (or anyone else) but still have complete management authority through their ownership of the general partner. All of the 98% in limited partnership interests can be gifted to others but control is maintained with just the 2% general partnership interest. (For more information on LPs and estate planning see my book: *How to Use Limited Liability Companies and Limited Partnerships* (SuccessDNA, 2016).)

To avoid later estate taxes a small amount of the limited partnership interest are gifted each year tax free to the next generation. The Wallops started gifting to their children and by 1998 WFLP was owned as follows:

Malcolm	41.625%
French	41.625%
Amy	2.95%
Oliver	2.95%
Malcolm M.	2.95%
Paul	2.95%
Scott	2.95%
WCR (GP)	2.00%

Amy, Oliver, Malcolm M. and Paul are Malcolm's children from his first marriage. Scott Goodwyn is French's son from an earlier marriage.

In April of 2000, Malcolm filed for divorce from French. Two years later the court awarded Malcolm all of French's interest in WFLP and WCR. Then, Malcolm's son Paul purchased a 50% interest in WCR, so that he and his father were the managers (through the corporate general partner) of WFLP. When Malcolm passed in September 2011, Paul, as trustee of Malcolm's trust, administered the other 50% WCR interest. Paul was then in sole control of WFLP.

Canyon Ranch had been used for ranching and recreational activities over the years. When WFLP was formed a lodge was built to provide guest rooms. In time, entities owned by Paul and sometimes Malcolm entered various use agreements with WFLP to provide bird hunting, big game hunting and other recreational services. Paul ran the side businesses and paid a fee to WFLP for the use of the property. As well, Paul and Malcolm also made contributions to keep the ranch going. To generate further survival monies, WFLP sold off parcels of its land (a scenario common to many Western ranches.) By 2011, Canyon Ranch was down to 2,860 acres.

Paul then offered to buy Scott's interest in WFLP. Malcolm and French had initially wanted to include her son Scott (who was not Malcolm's son) in all the gifting. But then the divorce happened. French was out of the picture and Scott was left behind with an interest in a family ranch where he wasn't 'family.' Attorneys will often counsel clients about gifting valuable property to non-family members. As things played out it is possible that patriarch Malcolm rued his decision.

Scott was initially interested in selling his WFLP interest but wanted an accounting to determine its value. After digging into it Scott and his advisors claimed to find accounting irregularities and evidence of mismanagement. In 2005, while Malcolm was still alive, Scott sued Malcolm and Paul individually as managers, as well as Paul's siblings Oliver, Malcolm M. and Amy, as limited partners of WFLP, for breach of fiduciary duty, breach of contract and breach of the covenant of good faith

Chapter Nine

and fair dealing. Scott also pursued a derivative claim on behalf of WFLP for these claims.[22]

Remember from our discussion in the last chapter, that a shareholder of a corporation, member of an LLC or limited partner of an LP can sue on behalf of the entity itself. The rationale is that those owners running the entity would never sue themselves. Accordingly, the courts allow an owner outside the inside circle of control to bring an action on behalf of the entity. This type of derivative claim is derived from a secondary source, the outsider seeking redress against wrongs committed within the entity that the insiders would never touch.

Or, as the Wyoming Supreme Court clearly stated in the Wallop case:

> Whenever a cause of action exists primarily in behalf of the corporation against directors, officers, and others, for wrongfully dealing with corporate property, or wrongful exercise of corporate franchises, so that the remedy should be legally obtained through a suit by and in the name of the corporation, and the corporation either actually or virtually refuses to institute or prosecute such a suit, then, in order to prevent a failure of justice, an action may be brought and maintained by a stockholder or stockholders, either individually or suing on behalf of themselves and all others similarly situated, against the wrongdoing directors, officers, and other persons. The stockholder does not bring such a suit because his rights have been directly violated or because the cause of action is his or because he is entitled to the relief sought; he is permitted to sue in this manner simply in order to set in motion the judicial machinery of the court. The stockholder, either individually or as the representative of the class, may commence suit, and may prosecute it to judgment; but in every other respect the action is the ordinary one brought by the corporation, it is maintained directly for the benefit of the corporation, and the final relief, when obtained, belongs to the corporation and not to the stockholder plaintiff. Where a suit by a limited partner against a general partner clearly alleges wrongs to the partnership which

The Wallop Case – Self Dealing?

have indirectly damaged the limited partner, the action asserts a derivative claim on behalf of the partnership, not one personal to the plaintiff.

Can you see how a derivative claim could be useful to you? Suppose you are in an investment where those in control are taking advantage of the situation. Their acts don't affect you directly. But because the company's performance does suffer, they affect you indirectly as an owner. It is important to know that you and the other passive owners can bring a derivative claim on behalf of the company. In most states you can be awarded attorney's fees if you succeed in court. Sometimes, just the mention of potential derivative litigation can get management back on track.

Alright, back to the Wallops. Scott sued his former step brothers and step sister as limited partners of WFLP. One can only imagine the dinner table conversations the Wallops had about this claim. Scott alleged that Oliver, Malcolm M. and Amy owed him fiduciary duties as limited partners, and claimed they should have taken steps to stop their brother and father from mismanaging the ranch.

The Wyoming Supreme Court swiftly shot down this argument:

> There is no common law duty owed by a limited partner to a general partner, the limited partnership, or other limited partners.

> To impose a duty upon a limited partner where none is provided under the WULPA [Wyoming Uniform Limited Partnership Act] would also defeat the purpose of forming a limited partnership. Limited partnerships provide limited partners the ability to be passive members of a partnership with limited liability and without imposing a duty upon the limited partners. The traditional purposes for imposing duties upon partners are absent in the limited partnership context. Imposing duties upon a limited partner would restrict a limited partner's benefits of a limited partnership.

Chapter Nine

As the Court correctly pointed out, the whole idea behind being a limited partner is to be limited in your financial exposure and your management authority. Requiring fiduciary duties of limited partners is wholly inconsistent with that whole idea.

Scott also claimed that Malcolm and Paul, as general partners of WCR, owed the duty of care, good faith and fair dealing to the other limited partners. Here he was on solid ground with the Wyoming Supreme Court. Such duties "...require that the general partner refrain from conducting business with the partnership, refrain from competing with the partnership, refrain from grossly negligent, reckless or intentional misconduct, and deal in good faith with the partnership and the limited partners."

Scott's claims dealt with self dealing, whereby a fiduciary takes advantage of their position and acts in their own self interest to the detriment of others. Self dealing can lead to a conflict of interest and a breach of fiduciary duties.

There were two entities controlled by Paul, and one by Malcolm, that did business with WFLP. No one denied this. "However, once a partner benefits his (or his entities') transactions with the partnership the burden then shifts to that partner – in this case the general partner, WCR – to demonstrate that no breach of duty has occurred."

The first entity was Elk Rock Companies, LLC, which was owned by Paul and his wife Sandra.

Prior to 2003, Canyon Ranch had been actively operated by a ranch manager. Part of this non-family manager's compensation was the ability to graze ten cows on WFLP land at no charge. When Paul took over as ranch manager he took as part of his compensation the same grazing rights, albeit for his 50 cows and another party's 50 cows. Was this rampant self-dealing, or a reasonable increase in Paul's compensation?

The second entity was Canyon Ranch Recreation, LLC, (CRR) owned by Paul and Malcolm, which entered into a bird hunting lease with WFLP. Before the lease with CRR, WFLP leased to Big Horn Canyon Ranch, Inc., (BHCR) a group of Washington lobbyists. BHCR paid WFLP over $190,000 a year in some years to hunt birds on the Canyon Ranch. Of course, besides hunting the lobbyists were also interested in getting to know and gain access to U.S. Senator Malcolm Wallop.

The 'game' is pay to play. However, for some reason when Senator Wallop retired and his influence waned in Washington, the lobbyists lost their interest in bird hunting. BHCR ended their lease.

Since no other company was interested in leasing the bird hunting rights, Paul and Malcolm formed CRR to continue the business. CRR operated from 2003 to 2011, when it was shut down due to a lack of business. Over the years CRR paid WFLP a total of $350,000 in lease payments but had a cumulative loss of $166,046. Paul and Malcolm did not greatly benefit from CRR. The court valued the opinion of the WFLP's accountant who testified that CRR eliminated the business risks to WFLP and did provide a stream of income for the limited partners.

After taking everything into consideration, the court found that the facts did not warrant a finding of a breach of any of the duties. They noted that WFLP's primary business purposes were achieved and that WCR acted in good faith.

Compare the facts in the Fredo case to the Wallop case. Fredo was clearly taken advantage of by Bruno. The facts are not so obvious with the Wallops. Paul and Malcolm lost money with their bird hunting CRR business. And that is a key factor in all of this. The facts matter. How you present the facts matters. The court knows all the standards for fiduciary duties and what to do if they are breached. The important challenge for you and your attorney is to apply the facts of the case in a way that the court can recognize a breach. Each decision will be dependent on the facts and how you present them as part of your story of wrongful conduct.

Scott also asserted that WCR's veil should be pierced to impose liability on Paul and Malcolm.

The Wyoming Supreme Court schooled the plaintiff: "...We do not consider veil-piercing until the threshold question of whether there is liability for an underlying cause of action has been answered."

You can't just pierce the veil without any entity wrongdoing. If duties were breached and the entity is liable then the question becomes: Can the entity pay the damages? If it can't, then you can try for the bull's–eye and

Chapter Nine

pierce the veil to get the owners to pay the damages. But first and foremost, the entity has to be liable for something. As we learned with King George, piercing can be painful. You don't do it without good reason.

The Court also schooled Scott on another facet of the case. If you want to impose liability on Paul and Malcolm, sue them for their actions within the company. Don't wait to try and pierce the veil to get at them later. Sue them personally right from the start. The court stated:

> Officers, directors and other agents may be held individually liable for personal participation in tortious acts even though performed solely for the benefit of the corporation, and such liability does not require that the "corporate veil" be pierced.

> However, it is necessary to pierce the corporate veil in order to impose personal liability upon a nonparticipating corporate officer. Participation sufficient to impose personal liability for tortious acts may consist of merely authorizing, directing, or voting for the acts, or knowing consent or approval...

> While an officer of a corporation cannot be held personally liable for a corporation's tort solely by reason of his or her official capacity, an officer may be held personally liable for his or her individual acts of negligence even though committed on behalf of the corporation which is also held liable...

> And the corporate veil need not be pierced where a tort action is brought against an officer or director and the elements of the tort are proved.

The Court stated that since no tort claims were brought directly against Paul and Malcolm it didn't need to "address that avenue of recovery."

Scott failed on all the claims involving breach of fiduciary duties and piercing. However, the Court did agree with him on the derivative claims, the ones he brought on behalf of the partnership. There were some outstanding partner loan debts and gifting issues which affected the whole partnership. The Court ordered that WFLP correct their books and tax records accordingly.

The Wallop Case – Self Dealing?

Because Scott prevailed on the derivative claims the court ordered WFLP to pay Scott's attorney's fees. As a result, Scott was not out the large amount of money spent on fighting the case. And during the long period of litigation, the value of ranch land in Wyoming increased significantly, as did the value of Scott's share in WFLP. So, while Scott lost on some claims, he gained on others in the long run.

As discussed, the Wallop case dealt with self dealing. When an officer, trustee, attorney or other fiduciary takes advantage of their position in a transaction to act in their own self interest (as opposed to the best interest of those they owe a duty to) the issue of self dealing can arise.

Self-dealing is a form of conflict of interest. You are acting in an official capacity to benefit your private interests, which conflicts with your fiduciary duties to others. Those others can sue to recover lost profits. In a charitable setting, repeated self-dealing can lead to a loss of tax-exempt status.

In the Wallop case, Paul used Elk Rock Companies, LLC, which he and his wife owned, to graze cattle on WFLP land. The rationale was that the previous ranch manager did the same. It was part of the compensation package, and Paul continued the practice when he took over as ranch manager. But whereas the previous ranch manager only grazed 10 of his own cows, Paul grazed 50 of his and allowed another 50 cows for a friend. Instead of 10, now there were 100. While Paul benefitted from this tenfold increase, WFLP received no benefit. One can easily see why Scott, the outsider, would be put off by this arrangement.

Taken by itself, the court may have found a self-dealing issue. But courts weigh all the factors. And another factor in the mix was Canyon Ranch Recreation, LLC, owned by Paul and Malcolm. CRR leased land from WFLP for bird hunting activities and paid $350,000 in lease payments to WFLP over the years. But over the years, until it was shut down for a lack of business, CRR suffered a cumulative loss of $166,046. It is hard to argue self-dealing in that scenario. Indeed, it can be argued that Paul and Malcolm did WFLP a favor by taking on such business work, risks and liabilities. And in the balancing that courts do, Paul's grazing gains were

Chapter Nine

offset by his bird hunting losses, thus minimizing the need for a finding of self-dealing.

Once again, the facts, and how you combine them, make all the difference.

And know that sometimes you can use the facts to get out of a case before it even goes to trial...

Chapter Ten

Summary Judgement – Getting out Quick

Why go all the way to trial if there aren't any key issues to begin with?

A summary judgment can be entered in favor of one party summarily, meaning without a full trial. Summary judgments save time and money and are granted when there are no disputes regarding the material facts of the case. Typically, you file a summary judgment motion at the start of a case before litigation gets expensive. Your plea to the judge is essentially: "There's no case here, your Honor. Let me out!"

In *Montana Engineering, Inc. v. Drake* [23] the court heard the case of a non-existent corporation.

It is very easy to pierce the veil of a corporation that did not bother to incorporate. As is clear for the judge, attorneys and everyone else to see, the veil never existed in the first place. (We will come back to this issue after reviewing the case.)

The question in the Montana Engineering case was which individual promoter of the phantom corporation would be held personally responsible for the engineering services that were actually performed.

Things started out innocently enough. Sam Richtofen and his firm Richtofen Architects, P.C. (collectively "Richtofen") represented Arnie Drake, who was doing business as Drake Corp. (collectively "Drake") There was topographical work to be done on a site in Shelby, Montana, which is 80 miles east of Glacier National Park and 30 miles south of the Canadian border. Richtofen authorized Montana Engineering to do the

Chapter Ten

work, stating in an email: "For now, you can invoice your time to my firm as listed below. This may change as things proceed on the project."

When Montana Engineering later emailed Richtofen an invoice for $19,610.86 the architect responded: "The owner would like you to bill him directly for your services." He then provided Montana Engineering with Drake's address in Aberdeen, South Dakota.

Unfortunately, Drake was unable to pay. Montana Engineering filed suit and when Drake didn't respond, the engineers obtained a default judgment.

A default judgment arises when the person being sued doesn't answer the plaintiff's complaint. An answer is a formal responsive pleading from the defendant stating that the plaintiff's allegations are wrong, inaccurate and/or without merit. The answer is a response that says "We're not liable." And it sometimes comes with a counter claim that says: "If anyone is liable it is the plaintiff, and for these reasons." With the answer on file the case gets into second gear. But if the defendant doesn't answer...

The plaintiff, after waiting 30 days (in most states) for an answer and receiving none, goes back into court. The attorneys essentially say to the judge: "Your Honor, they didn't respond. We should win the whole case by default." And in many cases the judge will grant a default judgment, meaning that the plaintiff has won solely because of the defendant's dereliction in not answering.

Now, in some cases, the defendant's attorneys can later go to the judge and say: "We're sorry, your Honor. We just received notice of the plaintiff's complaint. We didn't know about it until right now. Here's our answer. Can you revoke the default judgment so our clients can get a fair trial?" And in most cases the judge will lift the default judgment so the case can proceed.

But in some cases the defendant decides as a tactical matter not to answer at all. They know that a default judgment will be entered against them. But they don't care. The plaintiff can try and collect but there's no money to get. And by not answering the complaint they haven't spent whatever precious money they do have on attorney's fees. In this scenario a default judgment for the plaintiff can be as valuable as sleeves on a vest.

Summary Judgement – Getting out Quick

Montana Engineering, when it couldn't collect from Drake, then went after Richtofen and Mike Bright, who was also involved. Drake emailed the suing engineers:

> *I personally gave* these gentlemen the go ahead to request the survey based off of the information that I received from my investors. This is my investors' issue and mine only, not that of Mike Bright or Sam Richtofen ...In my opinion it is not accurate or legal to even begin to include them in this filing.

But Montana Engineering wanted to be paid. It filed a summary judgment motion against Richtofen claiming that the debt was really his. But the court couldn't see a crystal-clear issue of obligations. There wasn't a slam dunk issue of material facts for the court to justify a slambang summary judgment. So the Court denied Montana's motion for a quick out on a summary judgement victory.

Then Richtofen's attorneys reasoned: If the Court won't grant the engineers a summary judgment maybe they'll grant us one. Maybe the slam dunk is on our side of the case. Maybe there are no material facts to show that Richtofen is responsible for the debt.

Bingo.

In defending the motion Montana Engineering insisted it extended credit to Richtofen personally.

The engineers also claimed Richtofen was liable because he entered into the Montana Engineering contract on behalf of the Drake Corporation, which didn't exist.

What is the liability of the agent of a nonexistent corporation? The court set forth the law very clearly:

> ...Montana Engineering says Richtofen must pay because it said it was acting on behalf of "Drake Corporation" but no such corporation existed. It is true that an agent may be liable for contracts entered into on behalf of a nonexistent corporation... However, the reason for that rule is to assign the liability to the agent who, "although purporting to be acting for a principal, is in fact acting for himself." ...Montana Engineering does not allege or

Chapter Ten

prove that Richtofen was acting for itself. Drake's emails confirm that Richtofen was acting for Drake.

Montana Engineering's legal authorities for its fictitious-principal theory all involved fact patterns where the agent was effectively a corporate promoter who knew or should have known that no corporation actually existed. Ironically, the facts of the present case do include a person who was acting as a corporate promoter: Mr. Drake. A promoter like Mr. Drake who presumes to contract for a corporation that does not yet exist assumes the risk of personal liability. Drake knew the corporation he was promoting did not actually exist. The fictitious-principal rule is fair as applied to him. It is thoroughly irrational as applied to Richtofen.

When a court writes a last line like that you know you're going to win. After dismissing other Montana Engineering arguments, the court let Richtofen out of the case on summary judgment.

Let's go back to the issue of not having to pierce the veil of a corporation (like Drake's) which didn't exist. There are a few points to discuss.

First, you don't ever want to be in this position. You want to form your corporation or LLC right at the start and operate through it. Principals (like Drake) who operate as corporate promoters before the corporation is formed are personally liable for any corporate obligations. This is good public policy.

You don't want promoters hiding behind nonexistent entities.

Second, if you are the one extending credit and performing services you want to make sure the company exists. Do some due diligence. Go to the Secretary of State's website for the company's formation state and the states they are doing business in and check on their existence. Is the company real? Has the company been properly formed and paying its annual fees? Check the Better Business Bureau website and see what kind of reputation they have. If the company doesn't show properly maybe don't do business with them. Or get your fees upfront. Or get a personal guarantee. Mr. Drake, who unfortunately hadn't lined up his investors, may have balked at an upfront payment or personal guarantee and then

Summary Judgement – Getting out Quick

Montana Engineering wouldn't have been out the money. The entire case may never have happened.

Third, while you want to avoid litigation, if you are in it know this: In many states corporations that aren't current on their state filings cannot bring an action or defend themselves in court. Again, it is very important to pay the annual fees to the state you are formed in and the states you are qualified to do business in. You want to be able to legitimately access the court.

But what if the other side hasn't paid their fees? This would be a good time for a summary judgment motion. Your argument is that the 'company' is not entitled to bring an action or defend itself in court for a failure to pay the required fees. Understand that most judges generally want both sides to have their fair day in court. And so most judges will allow the company to pay the state fees and be properly before the court. But you knew that when you filed the summary judgment motion. You knew you may not win, at least initially. But it doesn't matter because you're laying a foundation for the second phase of action: Piercing the Veil.

When you've won a judgment against the company and it won't pay you want to be able to go against the individual owners. You want to show the court that the losing company doesn't follow the corporate formalities. Why not advance that argument early? The summary judgment motion for a failure to pay the required state filing fees plants that seed, which may bloom in the second phase of the case when you're actively aiming for the bull's-eye.

Of course, the law of your state does matter in all of this...

Chapter Eleven

Internal Affairs: Which State's Law Applies?

Which law applies when piercing the veil? The state of formation's law? Or the law of the state where the claim arose?

Bob forms a Nevada corporation and properly qualifies it to do business in California. So we have just one corporation that can do business in two states. Marisol does business with the corporation in California and now it owes her money. But the company has no more assets to pay her back, and she wants to hit the bull's-eye to get Bob's personal assets. Does California's weak law apply? That's where all the business was done. Or does Nevada's stronger law apply? That's where Bob intentionally set up the company. The issue may not seem important to you. Until you're hit with it.

The first way to deal with it all is to put it right up front in a contract. The contractual terminology is known as the Choice of Law and Venue provisions. The Choice of Law provision dictates which state law applies in the event of a dispute. The Choice of Venue provision sets forth in which court the case will be heard. Perhaps you have seen such a term, usually at the end of the contract:

"This contract shall be governed by the laws of the State of Nevada. Exclusive jurisdiction for any dispute shall be the Second Judicial District Court in and for the County of Washoe, State of Nevada. This is a mandatory venue selection clause."

That last sentence is important. You don't want anyone to challenge your home court advantage.

Chapter Eleven

Work with your attorney to include Choice of Law and Venue provisions that use state laws and court jurisdiction to your advantage.

Back to Bob and his dispute with Marisol in which there is no contract. The question remains: Is it fair for Bob to have to worry about which state law applies?

This is where the terms 'internal affairs doctrine' and 'conflict of laws principles' come into play which, especially the latter, are as welcome by most attorneys as acid reflux. Dean William L. Prosser, a legal giant of the last century, described it best: "The realm of the conflict of laws is a dismal swamp, filled with quaking quagmires, and inhabited by learned but eccentric professors who theorize about mysterious matters in a strange and incomprehensible jargon. The ordinary court, or lawyer, is quite lost when engulfed and entangled in it." [24]

The internal affairs doctrine within the conflict of laws morass attempts to bring order out of chaos.

Again, is it fair for Bob to have to worry about whether Nevada or California law applies to his case? The internal affairs doctrine holds that entities should not be subject to inconsistent legal standards. Instead, for the sake of the uniformity, certainty and predictability, only one state's laws should govern relationships between the corporation and its officers, directors and shareholders, otherwise known as their internal affairs. And since every entity has a state of formation (as opposed to other states it may later qualify to do business in) under the internal affairs doctrine, the law of the formation state applies.

Bob's wise choice to incorporate in Nevada means that Nevada law will apply in most cases. Interestingly (and not surprisingly), California is the one state that pushes back on the internal affairs doctrine.

California courts have held that their state has the greatest interest in certain litigation as opposed to, typically, Delaware, whose courts rail back at California's conflicts grab. Delaware, responding to a California decision, asserted that the internal affairs doctrine "serves the vital need for a single, constant and equal law to avoid the fragmentation of continuing, interdependent internal relationships."[25]

Internal Affairs: Which State's Law Applies?

The Delaware Supreme Court also stated in the same case:

"The umbilical tie of the foreign corporation to the state of its charter is usually religiously regarded as conclusive in determining the law to be applied in intracorporate disputes."

While certain skirmishes will still be fought between states the safe, general position (minus the exceptions ahead) is that the law of your state of incorporation will govern your internal affairs. Once again, Wyoming, Nevada and Delaware compete to be the best states for you.

What about in federal court? Is there a federal internal affairs rule? The answer is no.

Corporations are organized under state law and those laws apply to federal cases. The U.S. Supreme Court has stated that: "Except where federal law expressly requires certain responsibilities of directors with respect to stockholders, state laws will govern the internal affairs of the corporation."[26]

Will the law of the formation state apply in every single case? Unfortunately, not. In cases involving contract and tort obligations (which don't relate to internal affairs or corporate governance matters but are rather 'outside' the entity), we get back to the choice of law issues where there is an exception to every rule.

The 'learned but eccentric professors' Dean Prosser mentioned put together what are called Restatements of the Law. It is their way of giving back.

The Second Restatement of Conflicts of Law was put forth in 1969. Section 307 pertaining to "Shareholders' Liability," expressly provides:

"The local law of the state of incorporation will be applied to determine the existence and extent of a shareholder's liability to the corporation for assessments or contributions and to its creditors for corporate debts."

Since both the contract and tort obligations against a corporation are "corporate debts," the literal language of Section 307 appears to support the so-called "internal affairs doctrine". However, the provisions of Sections 301 and 302, as well as other relevant sections of the Restatement, make it clear (or at least murky) that Section 307 does not apply to all corporate veil piercing claims.

Chapter Eleven

Section 301, pertaining to "Rights and Liabilities to Third Persons," provides:

"The rights and liabilities of a corporation with respect to a third person that arise from a corporate act of a sort that can likewise be done by an individual are determined by the same choice-of- law principles as are applicable to non-corporate parties."

Thus, Section 301 does not automatically mandate the application of the law of the state of formation for issues relating to contract and tort obligations, including the issue of piercing the corporate veil. Indeed, Comment b to Section 301 draws a clear distinction between issues relating to the internal affairs of a corporation and issues relating to contract and tort obligations:

"Many acts can be done both by corporations and by individuals. Thus, corporations and individuals alike make contracts, commit torts and receive and transfer assets. Issues involving acts such as these when done by a corporation are determined by the same choice-of-law principles as are applicable to non-corporate parties...."

Yes. It is a dismal swamp. But we're almost out.

Likewise, Section 302, pertaining to "Other Issues with respect to Powers and Liabilities of a Corporation," provides:

"(1) Issues involving the rights and liabilities of a corporation, other than those dealt with in § 301, are determined by the local law of the state which, with respect to the particular issue, has the most significant relationship to the occurrence and the parties under the principles stated in § 6.

"(2) the local law of the state of incorporation will be applied to determine such issues, *except in the unusual case where, with respect to the particular issue, some other state has a more significant relationship to the occurrence and the parties, in which event the local law of the other state will be applied.*" (Emphasis added.)

Internal Affairs: Which State's Law Applies?

Thus, Section 302 does not absolutely mandate the application of the law of the state of formation for issues relating to contract and tort obligations, including piercing the corporate veil.

Well then, I think we've cleared things up. The law of the state of formation applies unless it doesn't. Still, it behooves you to form your entity in a state with strong, protective laws. You've lost the internal affairs argument if you incorporate in California or another weak state to begin with. Your argument is much stronger if, for example, you incorporate in Nevada for the benefit of her laws. Argue 'internal affairs' to get the most protection possible.

On the other hand, if you're trying to pierce the veil to get at someone's personal assets, you'll use the Restatement language we've just cited to your advantage. You want to be able to argue in favor of the weakest law possible. As the lawyers all know, you'll shape your arguments depending on which side you're on.

Internal Affairs and LLC Certification

Sometimes you can assert your internal affairs jurisdiction at the start. That is the strategy of 'certification.'

You want the best protection possible for your assets. You want to use the strongest entity available. But if you live in a weak asset protection state (like California) and set up your LLCs in a strong state (such as Wyoming), which state law applies? As we've learned in our discussion of the internal affairs doctrine, the old standard lawyer answer certainly applies: It depends.

If you live in California and hold your Wyoming LLC membership interest (your certificate representing ownership) in California, that certificate is your personal property in California. Your Wyoming LLC can then be subject to the jurisdiction of a California court. In such a case California's weaker laws will apply.

However, with some careful planning and by actually holding the physical Wyoming LLC certificates in Wyoming, the stronger asset

Chapter Eleven

protection of Wyoming law can apply. (Please note that we will use California and Wyoming in our discussion but any weak state/strong state scenario will apply.)

A membership interest in an LLC may be held in two ways: (1) as a certificated security; or (2) as an uncertificated security. A certificated security is a declared ownership interest (like a corporation's stock certificate) represented by a properly prepared and held certificate. An uncertificated security is an ownership that is ***not*** represented by a properly prepared certificate. *See*, UCC 8-102(4), (18). Too many cheap LLC promoters claim you don't need a certificate representing LLC ownership. This is a huge mistake.

1. Uncertificated Security

Most membership interests in LLCs are held as uncertificated securities. Indeed, a membership interest in an LLC is ***not*** a security, unless its terms expressly so provide. *See*, UCC 8-103(c).

One downside to holding an LLC as an uncertificated security is that it usually is considered by the courts to be a "general intangible." The courts see the LLC ownership as accompanying the owner of the uncertificated security. A court has jurisdiction over an individual if they live in the court's district. Personal jurisdiction means the court has the ability to assert orders against the individual. Thus, if a court in California has personal jurisdiction over a judgment debtor (someone who lost in court and for purposes of example we will call "Bob"), then the court in California also may have in rem (property) jurisdiction over Bob's Wyoming LLC. This is true even though his LLC was formed in Wyoming.

Bob's LLC membership interest is deemed to be "intangible personal property" that accompanies him in California. In this way, an uncertificated security representing a Wyoming LLC membership interest can be subject to California's weak laws. When Bob is served in a California collection case, a California court not only acquires personal jurisdiction over Bob but all of his California holdings as well, including uncertificated securities *even* if his LLCs were formed in Wyoming.

Neither Bob nor you wants this result. Let's consider a better alternative.

2. Certificated Security

There are distinct advantages to holding a membership interest in an LLC as a certificated security.

One definite advantage is that Bob's interest in a certificated security may be reached by a judgment creditor *only* by actual seizure of the security certificate by the officer making the attachment or levy. *See*, UCC 8-112(a). Thus, in dealing with certificated securities, possession of the securities is the vital matter. Placing them in a Wyoming safety deposit box, a service provided by our firm, Corporate Direct, puts the certificates out of the easy reach of a California (or other state) court.

Furthermore, the local law of the jurisdiction in which a security certificate is located at the time of delivery governs whether an adverse claim can be asserted against a person to whom the security certificate is delivered. *See*, UCC 8-110(c). Delivery of a certificated security occurs when the purchaser acquires possession of the security certificate. *See*, UCC 8-301(a)(1).

Therefore, if Bob acquires possession of a security certificate in Wyoming, then delivery of the security certificate occurs in Wyoming. As such, the law of Wyoming (the jurisdiction in which the security certificate was located at the time of delivery) governs whether an adverse claim can be asserted against Bob. In this way, even if Bob is served with process in California, the California court may apply *only* those stronger remedies against Bob's Wyoming LLC membership interest that exist in Wyoming, and *not* those weaker remedies that exist in California.

Thus, if a charging order against Bob's LLC membership interest is the exclusive remedy in Wyoming, a California court must apply Wyoming's superior law to the case. You control the internal affairs advantage.

Chapter Eleven

Corporate Direct has developed a method for certificating LLC securities in Wyoming to be governed by Article 8 of the UCC so that Wyoming law applies. We call it "Armor 8." We add specific jurisdictional Article 8 language to the Operating Agreement and the membership certificates. We hold the membership certificates in a safe deposit box at a Wyoming bank. Your certificates are physically located in Wyoming and governed by Wyoming law. We have not had a case challenging this procedure and can make no guarantees as to how any one court would rule. But by taking the extra steps here you are in a much better position to argue the applicability of Wyoming law, to your greater protection.

Use the internal affairs doctrine to your advantage.

Chapter Twelve

Clark Kent at Fault

In the world of veil piercing when Superman acts improperly his alter ego, Clark Kent, can be held responsible. Especially when Clark Kent sees to it that Superman is so poor he can't pay the claim.

That was the case in *BEQ, Inc. vs. Realty First, Inc.*[27] Realty First represented the sellers of a parcel of vacant land in San Clemente, California. BEQ was a real estate brokerage and management company for Tom and Terry Glen. The Glen family owned numerous real estate properties and used BEQ to manage them. When the Glens bought property for their own account, they used BEQ's real estate license to capture the buyer's side commission on each sale.

Except in the San Clemente deal. BEQ was buying the land for a future development. Realty First, on behalf of the seller, put the transaction together and was to receive the full commission. (Typically, in a sale of real estate the 5 or 6% broker sales commission is split in half – 50% to the selling agent and 50% to the buyer's agent. But in some cases, the selling or buyer's agent can receive both halves of the commission.)

BEQ alleged that they had a deal with Realty First to split the commission. When Realty First claimed back there was no such deal the case went to court. The trial court found that despite Tom and Terry's assertions, BEQ failed to prove the existence of a commission sharing agreement.

Realty First then sought to recover the $100,000 in attorney's fees the court awarded them. This is where the case went haywire.

Chapter Twelve

A total of four appeals were filed in the case before it was over. Each appeal can be another mini-trial. The attorney's fees surged, which provides us with two key lesson points at the end.

Earlier on, before the fourth appeal, Realty First sought to collect on their original judgment over BEQ. The judgment creditor (the winner of the case) can conduct a judgment debtor examination along with other discovery. At a debtor's exam the judgement creditor can ask all sorts of questions about the losing party's financial condition. Realty First called BEQ into court where under oath BEQ had to answer such questions.

At this hearing it came out that the Glens had already disposed of BEQ's assets and income. A levy of BEQ's bank accounts by Realty First, which is an allowed remedy for collection, would be useless.

It was also learned that just days after the court ordered BEQ to pay Realty First's attorney's fees and costs Terry set up a new corporation, CDR, Inc., also owned by the Glens. The family terminated all their property management contracts with BEQ and switched them over to CDR. The new company also took over the physical assets of BEQ. All of BEQ's former employees were now employed by CDR.

Clark Kent had deliberately impoverished Superman and had flipped the bird while doing it. In the fourth appeal Realty First argued under the alter ego doctrine that Tom and Terry were personally responsible for their claim against BEQ.

And so the Court of Appeals dug back into the case to determine if the alter ego test applied to Tom and Terry. The court started by reciting the Oakland Meat list (as was discussed in Chapter 4.) As later courts reviewed similar cases it had become clear that while not every factor on the Oakland Meat list has to be present for a piercing at least several of the factors should be.

Tom and Terry focused on how many factors **were not** present. They argued BEQ always took corporate minutes and always filed with the Secretary of State. They argued they never comingled assets and always maintained separate bank accounts. They asserted their business office was never used for personal business.

Clark Kent at Fault

While the court agreed that many Oakland Meat factors were missing, they clarified that wasn't really the issue. The issue was how many factors **were** present to establish the required unity of interest and ownership for an alter ego claim.

The ownership factor was present. They diverted assets away from BEQ (to the detriment of Realty First) to their new entity, CDR Inc., which was conveniently owned and controlled by the same family members.

The court also found that Tom and Terry treated BEQ's assets as their own. They didn't deal with BEQ at arm's length, which is legalese for social distancing. The individual and their entity must keep their distance, in their record keeping, banking and other affairs, to avoid the alter ego issue.

Specifically, once the commission dispute arose, Tom and Terry wanted the seller of the San Clemente property to reduce the sales price by the amount of BEQ's supposed commission. In real estate circles this is called 'commission in.' For example, a property is selling for $1,000,000 with a 5% commission. It is agreed that the seller's agent gets half – 2.5% or $25,000. The buyer is going to own the property. If the seller will reduce the purchase price by $25,000 (the buyer's half of the commission) the property then sells for $975,000. In this scenario the seller isn't out anything. He was going to net (after both commissions) $950,000 anyway. The buyer benefits because he doesn't have to come up with extra money for the full $1 million purchase price and the property taxes on a property valued at $975,000 (vs. $1 million) will be slightly lower. An even bigger benefit is that the buyer won't pay any earned income or payroll taxes on their $25,000 commission, which just disappears into a lower real estate acquisition price.

But in this case the seller had already agreed to pay Realty First the full commission. So to lower the purchase price by BEQ's supposed commission she would be losing money. She'd essentially be paying not a 5% commission but a 7.5% commission – a full price 5% commission to Realty First and another half to BEQ. Why would she do that?

The Court noted that this proposed transaction wouldn't benefit BEQ. Instead, it would only benefit Tom and Terry, the buyers of the San

Chapter Twelve

Clemente property. It was not to be done at arm's length, and another Oakland Meat factor was met.

The Court also noted some troubling corporate formality issues. Tom and Terry's mother had for years been listed as BEQ's registered (or resident) agent responsible for accepting government and legal notices for BEQ. Although she passed in 2010, she was listed as the resident agent for three more years. A formality of corporate formalities is the formal use of people who formally exist. Of course you can explain the matter away as an innocent mistake or as a way to keep Mom's memory alive but in this area of law (as in most areas of law) attention to detail matters. And the more details you miss...

Another detail had to do with BEQ's meeting minutes. Terry produced 47 pages of handwritten notes from meetings between 1992 and 2003. There were gaps, however.

As was learned, more handwritten notes had previously existed. But Terry's vacation motor home, where he had taken the notes to review several weeks before the judgment debtor examination, had caught fire. Certain handwritten notes of meetings had been burned in the vehicle fire and were forever lost. Terry provided a police report indicating that a faulty battery inverter had caused the fire. This incident may have been completely innocent. It is interesting that the court flatly mentioned the fire it in its write up of the case without further comment. Sometimes no commentary is necessary.

Was there an inequitable result? The court found there was.

There are cases where a corporation simply can't pay its bills. And there are cases where the owners deliberately ensure that the corporation can't pay its bills, where Clark Kent renders Superman powerless. Tom and Terry stripped BEQ of all its assets and business opportunities and moved them over to CDR. BEQ was left penniless days after the court ordered BEQ to pay over $750,000 to Realty First's attorneys for their fees. Tom and Terry's actions, the court easily found, were in bad faith.

Moving assets among related entities to evade the payment of obligations, especially court ordered ones, is the kind of inequitable conduct, a badge of fraud as found in Appendix A, that justifies an alter ego ruling.

The court held Tom and Terry personally responsible. They failed their veil.

At the start we said there were two lesson points about attorney's fees. First, the court originally awarded $100,000 in attorney's fees. By the end, after four appeals, the fees were over $750,000.

Tom and Terry hid assets to avoid paying attorney's fees. Attorneys don't like that. Like a dog with a bone they will tenaciously pursue what is owed them. Realty First was owed something, but the lion's share was owed to the attorneys. You don't want to become their target. And you don't want to compound your problems by hiding assets to avoid paying unrelenting attorneys.

Piercing the veil cases can be difficult for business owners. They are less difficult for attorneys who are owed a lot of money.

The second point has to do with Tom and Terry's side of the case. Why did Realty First's attorney fees rise from $100,000 to over $750,000? Who was guiding the decisions on the Glen family's side to keep moving forward? The principals or the attorneys? How much did BEQ and the Glens have to pay in attorney's fees on their side of the case through the four appeals? Another $750,000? Maybe more?

And so we have a case involving a disputed real estate commission in which perhaps over $1.5 million was spent in attorney fees. This is not a wise allocation of resources.

While without any knowledge of the inside particulars of the BEQ case, I have witnessed cases over the years in which attorneys fees have been allowed to surge. As a business owner you have to be very careful that you are not lured into this scenario. Some attorneys (not all – but some) will encourage you to fight for your 'principles'. You will be buoyed into confronting those who have taken advantage of you and must be taught a lesson as to what is fair and right and just. You will be emboldened to fight the good fight. And you will be goaded into the legal arena by someone who benefits whether you win or lose.

Chapter Twelve

When an attorney encourages you to fight for your principles grab your wallet. Think about it carefully. Ask others for advice. Do you really want the emotional strain and financial drain of litigation?

Most of us do not.

Chapter Thirteen

Two Companies – One Owner
A Bull's–eye or a Miss?

One standard for piercing the corporate veil involves one person serving as the management for two separate companies. When the separateness ceases to exist between several companies and their one officer problems can arise. When a president operates the two companies as one entity by commingling assets and conducting operations from the same office, courts have disregarded the corporate structure and pierced the veil. But even with similar facts it doesn't happen every time. Let's look at several separate but somewhat comparable cases.

In a Texas case [28] Debby Davis had her right index finger crushed when a clamp press malfunctioned. She sued Zebu Instruments Corporation ("Zebu") for its failure to provide a safe workplace. She also sued Robert Lake, as the responsible officer of both Zebu and Lynx Management, Inc., ("Lynx") which may have been Davis's true employer.

The key evidence in the case was an OSHA citation indicating that Zebu was responsible for maintenance of the press and that Zebu owed a duty to Davis to provide a safe workplace.

But while finding against Zebu the court couldn't hold Mr. Lake or Lynx at fault. The court wrote:

> As for Lake, we conclude that there was no evidence to support a finding that he is subject to individual liability. Corporations are separate legal entities from their shareholders, officers, and directors, who may not be held personally liable to obligees of the corporation absent a showing that they caused the corporation

Chapter Thirteen

to be used for the purpose of perpetrating and did perpetrate an actual fraud for direct personal benefit...

This "piercing the corporate veil" may be accomplished by the theory of the alter ego, which may be applied if there is a unity between the corporation and the individual to the extent the corporation's separateness has ceased, and holding only the corporation liable would be unjust...

As proof of alter ego, courts may consider (1) the payment of alleged corporate debts with personal checks or other commingling of funds; (2) representations that the individual will financially back the corporation; (3) the diversion of company profits to the individual for his personal use; (4) inadequate capitalization; and (5) other failure to keep corporate and personal assets separate...

An individual's standing as an officer, director, or majority shareholder of an entity is, in and of itself, insufficient to support a finding of alter ego.

The issue of two companies, Zebu and Lynx, both operated by Lake, was not material. The duty to Davis was owed by Zebu, and Lake did not somehow benefit from her injury.

In a similar New York case[29] the court reached a very different decision. The facts, however, are more extreme.

Dallas Powder sold explosives to Bi-State Construction Supply, Inc. ("Bi-State") which in this transaction didn't pay the bill. Dallas sued Bi-State and was awarded a judgment of $118,169.18. Bi- State cried poor, claiming they had no money to pay off the judgment.

Dallas called their bluff and sought to collect from Bob McKay individually and from Renfro Inc. ("Renfro"). McKay owned and operated both Bi-State and Renfro.

The facts revealed a tangled mess of no separateness. Explosives were delivered to a trailer owned by McKay and parked next to his residence. The explosives were then driven by a Renfro employee in a Renfro truck (which bore a Bi-State logo) to the end user. Renfro paid for the trailer owned by

Two Companies – One Owner

McKay and used the trailer as its office, as did Bi-State. Renfro also paid for McKay's Porsche car payment and Bi-States' phone bills. Bi-State had a checking account that paid for Renfro's payroll and management fees as well as McKay's golf club dues.

To complete the lack of business formality, it was learned that neither Renfro nor Bi-State ever held any corporate meetings or prepared any corporate records. Both companies were solely owned by McKay as his alter ego. He did whatever he wanted whenever he wanted. As the court found:

> ...it is clear from the record that McKay operated Bi-State and Renfro as one entity by commingling assets, conducting operations from the same office and paying management fees to Renfro from Bi-State which served to divert these funds away from Bi-State's creditors, confirming plaintiff's contention that the two corporations were inextricably intertwined and justifying a disregard of the corporate structure.
>
> When a corporation has been so dominated by an individual or another corporation and its separate entity so ignored that it primarily transacts the dominator's business instead of its own and can be called the other's alter ego, the corporate form may be disregarded to achieve an equitable result.

Many clients have wondered over the years what is wrong with using the same office for two corporations. Many have been sold expensive office packages by corporate promoters to offset this 'problem.' Beware of this come-on because the answer to the shared office question is there is nothing wrong with it. If you do it right. Related businesses do it all the time, but in McKay's case, Renfro paid the mortgage payments on the trailer and used the trailer as its corporate office. Bi-State also used the trailer as its office but did not pay anything. That's not how real business works. Bi-State should have paid to Renfro its fair share of the office expense. Bi-State, instead of Renfro, should have paid its own telephone bills. The commingling of business expenses between corporate bodies paints an unfortunate and blurry picture of one entity when you want

Chapter Thirteen

a clear presentation of two or more entities operating independently. The shared office issue can be overcome by proper accounting, sub-lease agreements and other documentation. Don't be sold an office package you don't really need.

What about McKay using the companies for his Porsche and golf club payments? Your creative CPA may have an argument that these are legitimate business expenses. Your excellent CPA may be able to convince the IRS of their legitimacy.

But you are far from the Tax Code in a piercing case. You are now in the court of public opinion.

For judge and jury, many of whom do not have the luxury of smooth CPAs backing up fine company cars and swanky memberships as business expenses, appearances are all important.

Again, the facts matter. If you and your team have done everything possible to follow the corporate formalities and your only 'sin' is a Porsche payment you should be okay. In McKay's case none of the required formalities were followed. And in that scenario, a Porsche payment may lead a creditor straight to the bull's–eye.

Can a non-owner of a company be held personally liable on a piercing claim?

A recent Idaho case[30] is instructive on this important issue. Thomas Lundemo was hired as the Chief Operating Officer for Mary Friendly Life Corp., ("MFL"), an Idaho multi-level marketing company that sold memberships for discount travel accommodations.

Bob Edmonds was the sole shareholder of MFL. His wife Sherry was not an owner but worked as the COO before Lundemo came aboard and was MFL's Executive Vice President afterwards.

Bob had hired Lundemo because he'd had experience at CeleFresh, which developed nutritional products. If you already have the multi-level marketing infrastructure for sales in place, nutritional products are a great source for growth.

102

Two Companies – One Owner

At some point, based on the 'false rumor' that Lundemo was contractually prohibited by CeleFresh from developing nutritional products for others, Bob fired Lundemo. MFL's employment agreement with Lundemo stated that if he were terminated without cause six month's salary, or $60,000, was due. Lundemo sued MFL for the $60,000, which Idaho wage laws tripled to $180,000.

Faced with such a judgment, Bob and Sherry drained MFL of its assets. Lundemo then sought to pierce the corporate veil and hold Bob and Sherry personally liable for the $180,000 judgment against MFL.

As in other cases, MFL never prepared annual minutes. There were no written documents evidencing the transfer of funds between companies.

The key question in the case was could Sherry, who was neither a shareholder, director or major officer, be held personally responsible for the claim? Sherry's attorneys argued adamantly that her separate property assets, which must have been the real source for any reward, should not be exposed to the MFL claim since she did not own the company.

The Idaho court had no problem in clearly answering:

> While Sherry Edmonds was not a shareholder, she certainly received all financial benefits from being married to the sole shareholder. More important than the fact that Sherry Edmonds benefits by being married to the sole shareholder, is the fact that Sherry Edmonds' own actions made her husband's financial remuneration so great, and conversely, her own actions made MFL judgment-proof. Sherry Edmonds testified at length at the trial about her involvement in the financial operations of all the businesses she and Bob Edmonds owned, but especially, MFL. Part of the reason Bob Edmonds had an incredibly large $265,684.00 shareholder distribution from MFL for 2014, the year Lundemo worked for MFL for two months on top of the $368,000,00 in credit card purchases from MFL, was because Sherry Edmonds made it that way. She was the one moving money around. Part of the reason MFL later became judgment-proof is because $87,500 went from MFL to TenCorp and Downieville

Chapter Thirteen

Signs, (related entities) and never came back to MFL. That was due to Sherry Edmonds' actions. There are other reasons MFL became prematurely judgment-proof. Those reasons are also due to Sherry Edmonds' actions.

And to sum up its thinking the court stated:

There are many ways to organize a sham corporation. In some instances, the wrongdoer neither holds stock nor serves in an official capacity.

Making officer, director, or shareholder status a prerequisite to veil piercing elevates form over substance and is therefore contrary to veil-piercing's equitable nature.

Speaking of substance, it is interesting to note that at one point the ruling stated that Bob and Sherry were not 'credible witnesses.' This is polite court-speak for: The judge didn't believe a word they said.

It is a lesson for us all. When you go to court you are under oath to tell the truth. That is your obligation. But it is more important than that. When the judge knows you aren't telling the truth, bad things can happen.

Know that judges possess excellent BS detectors. Next to U.S. Secret Service agents they are best at seeing through falsehoods and misrepresentations. And though you'll never notice any outward signs of it, they get mad when you try to bullshit them. And when they're mad, they can order a company's non-owner held personally liable for a piercing claim.

Chapter Fourteen

The Communist Takeover Case

The alter ego doctrine has been used in some unique cases. None was more unusual than when the Communist Party in California tried to use alter ego to take over the assets and property of two other corporations. The Communists alleged they had a secret agreement for the takeover. For context, in 1917 the Bolsheviks led by Vladimir Lenin had a secret agreement amongst themselves to take over control of the entire Russian economy and nation. This was not known to the average Russian at the time. The outcome was catastrophic. Read Alexander Solzhenitsyn's *The Gulag Archipelago* to learn of the resulting horrors of a Communist takeover.

Back to California. The case started in the Superior Court for the City and County of San Francisco. The judge in that case agreed with the Communist Party that by virtue of secret agreements they were the true owners of the two valuable corporations. The judge ordered the defendants to transfer all of the corporation's assets, which were declared held in a constructive trust, to the Communists.

As previously mentioned, a constructive trust is created by operation of law, meaning it automatically springs to life by court order under certain circumstances. This type of trust is used as a remedy to compel the transfer of property from the people wrongfully holding it to the rightful owners. For a constructive trust to exist there must be evidence that both the property was wrongfully acquired by someone not entitled to possession and there is some other party rightfully entitled to that property.

Chapter Fourteen

Constructive trusts spring to life in estate matters. Grandma passes, daughter takes over her assets but grandson, under the clear terms of the will, is entitled to them. A constructive trust is imposed by court order so daughter does not unjustly enrich herself or take advantage of her own wrongdoing.

But when it comes to Communists and secret agreements leading to constructive trusts and asset seizures the appellate court above the county court said: Let's reconsider this one!

In *Communist Party of the United States of America v. 522 Valencia, Inc.,*[31] the California Court of Appeals, as an appellate court often does, reviewed the whole case all over again.

The case involved two corporations. The first, 522 Valencia, Inc., owned valuable real estate in San Francisco which the Communists had rented for their offices. The second, Pacific Publishing, Inc., published *People's World*, a "working class, Marxist oriented newspaper." Ironically, Pacific Publishing was now defending itself from a Marxist takeover.

The gist of the Communists' argument was "that it was *entitled* to ownership of these assets." Because party members provided funding for the two companies "it was reasonable to infer that it was entitled to possession" of all the assets under the alter ego doctrine.

The appellate court shot down the Communists' argument. They clarified that:

> ...Alter ego is used to prevent a corporation from using its statutory separate corporate form as a shield from liability only where to recognize its corporate status would defeat the rights and equities of third parties; it is not a doctrine that allows the persons who actually control the corporation to disregard the corporate form.
>
> In this case, respondent has always treated both Valencia and Pacific Publishing as corporations legally separate from itself. It paid rent, borrowed money, entered into contracts and agreements, corresponded with, and generally dealt with both appellant corporations as though they were separate corporate entities. There is no evidence in the record of any disregard of

The Communist Takeover Case

corporate form or legal formalities. To the contrary, respondent always carefully maintained a legal separation between itself and the corporate appellants.

Respondent now contends, however, that the individual appellants had a secret agreement with the Party to manage the appellant corporations for the Party's benefit, rather than for the purposes stated in the corporations' own articles of incorporation. As part of this purported contract, the appellants allegedly agreed that all corporate decisions would be made by the Party rather than the nominally independent boards of directors of the corporations. Respondent argued that the "[directors] did exactly what the Party told them; they cooperated with the Party, and they served as ...Board of Directors' members without independently exercising their judgment."

A contract purporting to delegate ultimate authority and control over a corporation from the board of directors to outside parties with no ownership interest in the corporation is a contract that is void and unenforceable.

Agreeing with the Communists' arguments would lead to extremely bad precedent. If you had enough partisan 'witnesses' to claim that one corporation was intended to be owned by another, contrary to the written corporate documentation, what kind of litigation would ensue?

It wouldn't be pretty. Or fair.

The appellate court stated that alter ego was used to prevent two parties with similar interests from using the corporate form to harm an independent third party. But in this case there was no third party. Instead there were two separate parties with opposing interests – the Communists wanted control of Valencia and Pacific, and Valencia and Pacific didn't want to be taken over. Allowing alter ego to smother the rights of opposing entities was not to be tolerated.

The court also noted that: "Respondent cannot use the alter ego doctrine to "pierce the corporate veil" of a separate corporation which it

Chapter Fourteen

claims it set up to conceal its property from the federal government and to circumvent the laws of the state concerning duties of corporate directors."

The court's statement raises the issue of unclean hands (sometimes called the clean hands doctrine). A party seeking judgment cannot be helped by the court if they have acted unethically. When a party has acted in bad faith – that is, with unclean hands – the court will not reward them. The doctrine is often stated as "equity must come with clean hands."

In this case, if the Communists set up the two corporations in bad faith as a way to conceal their ownership from the federal government they can't later go into court and essentially say "Okay, we'd like our assets back now."

The courts will not help Communists or anyone else acting in bad faith.

Chapter Fifteen

The Wizard of Oz in Connecticut

The last time we saw the Wizard of Oz he was manipulating Emerald City for his own benefit. He was creating the instrumentality rule by dominating the city apparatus and then using that control to breach a duty and commit a wrong. The third step for the Wizard's rule to become actionable was that his absolute control and breach of duty must have caused an injury. Under the right circumstances, the Wizard's veil will be pierced.

The state of Connecticut likes the instrumentality rule evidenced by the Wizard of Oz. (They are less keen on Superman's alter ego, Clark Kent.) However, in Connecticut, courts have wrestled with the instrumentality rule. Despite scheming machinations and dominations, the Wizard isn't always held liable in Connecticut, as our next two cases will illustrate.

Our first case[32] involves Black Gold Paving, Inc., a union contracting company owned by Vinny Flat. Vinny also owned DGM Inc., a construction equipment leasing company. Vinny knew the business. Black Gold employed Artie and Arnie, both of whom really needed and appreciated their jobs.

One day, Vinny called the two young men into his office. "Boys," said Vinny, "we're creating a non-union shop and here's how it's going down." Vinny said the union pension obligations were killing him and that he was losing business to all the new non-union shops. Since he knew all the union big wigs, both professionally and socially, Vinny's name would have to be kept out of things.

109

Chapter Fifteen

Vinny then explained that he was forming a new contracting company called Scabbard Paving, Inc. Artie and Arnie, in name only, would be Scabbard's president and secretary-treasurer. (They would flip a coin for their positions). Vinny made it very clear that Artie and Arnie would be following his lead. "No one needs to get a big head over this," said Vinny.

Artie and Arnie, fearful of losing their jobs at Black Gold or wherever Vinny wanted them to work, agreed to the arrangement.

Two weeks later, Vinny invited the two to his attorney's office. In a plush conference room, the attorney and Vinny sat in expensive leather chairs. As a reminder, Artie and Arnie were shone to less expensive chairs that were six inches lower than the other two.

The attorney announced that this was the organizational meeting of Scabbard Paving, Inc. When Artie asked if an attorney should represent them Vinny glared and told them to just sign the documents. The two men did, and the attorney congratulated them on being the officers and directors of the new company.

"Now for the stock," said Vinny. The lawyer pushed forth two promissory notes. "I'm loaning each of you $5,000 and you are using that to buy your stock in Scabbard." They did as they were told and signed.

After all was done, Vinny was not an officer, director or shareholder of Scabbard Paving, Inc. A few weeks later another agreement was entered into. Scabbard was going to lease all the construction equipment they needed from DGM, Inc., Vinny's leasing company. In exchange, Vinny was going to get 25% of Scabbard's net profits until he received $300,000. After that, Vinny would receive 60% of the profits and Artie and Arnie would each receive 20%. Of note, Vinny wasn't an owner of Scabbard (and thus not entitled to dividends) but he did have the option to buy a majority of the shares if he wanted to someday.

Vinny said he had arranged for all the necessary bonding. Artie and Arnie were told to go get bids on projects. On an early job Artie and Arnie needed concrete and crushed stone. Since Scabbard was a new company without a credit history, Thompson Supply, Inc. required a personal guarantee of the president and treasurer. Artie and Arnie signed the guarantees, making them personally liable if Scabbard couldn't pay.

110

The Wizard of Oz in Connecticut

Scabbard couldn't pay. Thompson sued Artie and Arnie for the money. Artie and Arnie finally met with a business litigator who, to be even, was lividly surprised by the entire arrangement. The attorney suggested that if anyone was responsible for the personal guarantee it was Vinny, and Vinny was brought into the lawsuit as a new third party defendant.

The Connecticut Supreme Court set forth their standard:

> The instrumentality rule requires, in any case but an express agency, proof of three elements: (1) Control, not mere majority or complete stock control, but complete domination, not only of finances but of policy and business practice *in respect to the transaction attacked* so that the corporate entity as to this transaction had at the time no separate mind, will or existence of its own; (2) that such control must have been used by the defendant to commit fraud or wrong, to perpetrate the violation of a statutory or other positive legal duty, or a dishonest or unjust act in contravention of plaintiff's legal rights; and (3) that the aforesaid control and breach of duty must proximately cause the injury or unjust loss complained of. (Original italics left in place).

The Court then noted this wasn't your normal piercing case where a creditor was "suing an individual who has used a corporation as an instrument of fraud." Instead, said the Court, "this unique situation presents us with an attempt by an insider to pierce the corporate veil to reach an "outsider" who, personally and not through another corporate entity, exercises a great deal of control over corporate affairs."

The Court didn't have a problem with Vinny not being an officer, director or shareholder. The issue for piercing was the amount of control and influence exercised by the individual sought to be held liable.

The signing of the personal guarantees by Artie and Arnie, as the evidence showed, did not involve Vinny. He didn't ask Artie and Arnie to sign them, and didn't even know about the transaction (which is why the court highlighted the words "in respect to the transaction attacked" in their standard.) Instead, the record revealed that Artie and Arnie signed the guarantees voluntarily.

Chapter Fifteen

Whatever Vinny's role had been with regard to the other corporate actions, it couldn't be held that Scabbard was a mere instrumentality or agent of Vinny in connection with the signing of the guarantees. "The fact," said the Court, "that the corporate veil could be disregarded for some purposes does not mean that it must be disregarded for all purposes."

One Justice wrote a blistering dissent, and put forth even more evidence of Vinny's enveloping influence over Scabbard. From its cradle to its grave, the justice wrote, Scabbard was under the total control of Vinny.

The majority of the justices are, of course, aware of any dissenting opinions. And so the majority decision states: "While the result we reach in this case may seem harsh, this court does not and cannot rescue a party from its own unfavorable or unwise business dealings. A hard bargain is not enough to energize the equitable power to disregard the corporate form."

It is at this point we need to consider what justices at supreme and appellate courts all over the country must wrestle with. First of all, their decisions set precedent for cases to come. They know their decisions today will be the basis for future decisions, and they also know that at some point in time their decisions may be overruled by different scenarios, facts or changing public attitudes. But for the here and now, they try to get it right within the framework of existing cases. Case law is a jigsaw puzzle and the judges try their best to make the pieces fit.

There is a second concern the judges wrestle with. Their decisions set standards. Not only legal standards but behavioral standards. Judges help guide the way for how all of us interact. And in this case, Artie and Arnie voluntarily signed a personal guarantee. That is a key step in the business ecosystem. Businesses extend credit when individuals are willing to be personally responsible for their company obligations.

To let Artie and Arnie off the hook could diminish an important business standard that everyone should know: You don't sign a personal guarantee unless you are willing to be held liable for the debt. The economy flows when people are willing to take risks. It suffers when people attempt to avoid their obligations to the detriment of others.

The Wizard of Oz in Connecticut

While the facts in this case were close (especially given the dissent's recounting of them) the standard for others to follow is important. Will you be able to avoid a voluntarily entered into obligation by blaming others? For the Connecticut Supreme Court, the answer was: No.

Nevertheless, under the right circumstances, the Wizard of Oz can still be held liable in Connecticut.[33] Ron Resim was a British accountant who worked as an executive for large American corporations. He formed Viewcrest LLC to own two large apartment buildings outside Mystic, Connecticut. Resim was the sole owner of Viewcrest and managed all of its affairs, including lining up electricity service from Connecticut Light and Power Company ("the Power Company").

In an effort to keep its citizens always warm during brutally cold winters (and so politicians could look good against giant enterprises) the state of Connecticut had put forth statutes and regulations that made collection somewhat difficult for the Power Company. They were prohibited from requiring their customer to post a security deposit. They couldn't require a personal guarantee from their customer. And worst of all, for them, the Power Company couldn't shut off the power to customers who didn't pay their bills.

For all the feel-good fairness of keeping the elderly from freezing, there are people such as Ron Resim who view fairness as weakness and take advantage of it. Resim knew that the power Company's remedies against him were limited to one. The Power Company could go to court and seek the appointment of a receiver of rents, a person designated to go to the apartments, stand in for Resim and physically collect the rents until the power bill was satisfied. This single remedy was a royal pain.

As the Court stated, power companies are reluctant to pursue this 'remedy' because it is:

> expensive, time-consuming, confusing to the tenants, causes tenants to stop paying rent to anyone and can result in the electric utility becoming in effect the manager of the building. Accordingly, companies such as the plaintiff, when dealing with a nonpaying owner, use the receivership process only as a last resort.

Chapter Fifteen

Resim knew this. He took ownership of the apartments in May of 2000 and didn't pay a bill until August. Even then, it was only a partial payment. Resim's September 2000 bill was over $11,000 and he didn't pay again until March, 2001. The Viewcrest account history was filled with demands for payment and unfilled promises for payment.

The Power Company finally had enough. In May, 2002 their attorney demanded payment in full by June 4, 2002 or the application for a receiver of rents would be filed.

Resim sold his apartments on June 3rd. At that point, Viewcrest owed the Power Company over $46,000 for services it actually received. When the Power Company's attorneys demanded payment, Resim said it was an LLC obligation that couldn't be paid.

The Power Company went to Court to invoke the instrumentality rule and pierce the veil. The Court had no problem doing so. It found that Resim:

> Was not a credible witness; his testimony was inconsistent, evasive and contradicted by much other evidence, including his deposition. The court further found that he was the sole owner, member and manager of Viewcrest which he formed for the sole purpose of owning the two buildings in question. His residence was Viewcrest's principal place of business. He was in total control of all of Viewcrest's operations and made all the decisions involving finances, policy and business practices. No state or federal tax returns were filed by Viewcrest for the three tax years that Viewcrest owned the buildings, and he intentionally failed to preserve Viewcrest's financial records so that there was inadequate documentary support for his claim that Viewcrest was a losing venture. Resim's control and domination of all of Viewcrest's affairs was such that as to the obligation to the plaintiff, Viewcrest had no separate mind, will or existence of its own.

The Wizard of Oz in Connecticut

Resim's attorney, as he was paid to do, argued that the veil shouldn't be pierced just because Resim was the sole owner of the company. The debt belonged to Viewcrest and the formation and operation of an LLC should be respected to protect Resim.

The court would have none of it.

> ...We reject the defendant's suggestion that this was simply a case of a single shareholder being charged with a corporate debt solely because of his ownership status. There was ample evidence that Viewcrest had no separate existence, that Resim treated it as such and that Resim used it to perpetrate an unjust act in contravention of the plaintiff's legal rights. The evidence in this case amply supports the court's determination that the corporate veil should be pierced.

There is no record of Resim, like the Wizard of Oz before him, avoiding the consequences by sailing off in a hot air balloon to Kansas.

Chapter Sixteen

Undercapitalization

One of the more confusing standards for veil piercing is undercapitalization. Not having enough capital in the business can be grounds for a piercing. Of course, you want businesses to be able to meet their obligations. But a myriad of conflicting questions arise when considering how much capital is required.

Is it unfair to creditors for the company to operate without at least some minimal level of capital to survive in the business they are in? Should businesses, like Mr. Drake's in Chapter 10, enter into contracts if they can't pay for the services or goods at that moment? Or, on the other hand, is it the creditors' responsibility to check on the entity's solvency? If creditors are concerned, they can always do credit checks and/or request a personal guarantee from the individual owners before providing anything of value. That seems prudent. And yet there are some businesses which misrepresent their financial standing. But, as our rhetorical tennis match continues, just how careful do you want to be? Most businesses do pay their bills.

Into this back and forth confusion is added statutory minimum capitalization. Texas, for example, requires that each new entity be capitalized with at least $1,000. That amount barely covers all your start-up costs. Are you properly capitalized with just $1,000 at the start? Probably not, especially if you will next enter into contracts valued at tens of thousands of dollars.

Chapter Sixteen

Other questions arise: Is the term 'undercapitalized' too narrow? Capital may be only one element of a company's worth. Other assets besides just money, including credit lines, plant and equipment and intellectual property, may allow a business to operate properly. Harvey Gelb, a professor at the University of Wyoming College of Law, has argued that the question should be framed as to whether the entity has operated with an "inadequate level of assets." Gelb wrote "...the analysis should focus on whether the corporation has been provided with an inadequate level of assets to meet the type of claim involved."

And then the next question arises: Is undercapitalization (or an inadequate level of assets) frozen in time? Does it only apply to the corporation at its founding and first days in business? Or is it a moving standard whereby the business's capital requirements change as it grows and enters into larger transactions? Is undercapitalization fixed at inception or open-ended forever? Should the shareholders of a corporation, who properly funded it at the start, be personally punished when the entity runs into liquidity problems later?

Good luck with these questions. Others have wrestled with them before you.

We will next discuss several cases that hopefully shed some light on undercapitalization.

In *Waco Securities vs. Banco Dollar, Inc.*[34] the brokerage firm ("Waco") had first obtained a multimillion-dollar judgment against Roop Corporation ("Roop") for failing to pay margin debt, sued to collect the judgment debt, both by piercing the corporate veil to hold the corporation's insiders personally liable on the judgment debt, and by setting aside certain transfers of corporate assets. When companies transfer monies to insiders to avoid paying outsiders the court has the power, because the transfer was fraudulent, to order the money back.

The United States District Court for the Northern District of Illinois found Roop's insiders to be personally liable and voided certain transfers as fraudulent. Roop and the insiders appealed. The Seventh Circuit noted that Waco shrewdly had raised veil piercing and fraudulent transfer claims in order to recoup about $1.9 million in margin debt from a group

118

Undercapitalization

of businessmen once dubbed "The Bad Boys of Winnetka Arbitrage," and found this to be a particularly compelling case, because the District Court's generally undisputed findings – a convoluted web of entities, insider transactions, and sham loans all designed to avoid financial responsibility – soundly supported Waco's claims.

The three Bad Boys of Winnetka Arbitrage, whom we'll call Timmy, Tommy and Don, were sharp operators. Together they set up Roop Corp. for their real estate holdings. Banco Dollar, Inc. (Banco) was owned by Timmy's family trust and it extended a line of credit to Roop. In exchange, Roop granted Banco a blanket lien over all of Roop's assets. A promissory note and security agreement documented the deal. In a real estate setting we call this type of transaction equity stripping, whereby Roop's equity is stripped and secured in favor of Banco. As we counsel our clients, you can't hope to succeed with this if you are furthering anything improper. But the Bad Boys went forward with it.

On the same day, several Roop subsidiaries entered into a participation agreement on the Banco line of credit whereby $3 million was advanced by the subsidiaries to Roop. The subsidiaries, in return, were granted senior secured creditor status over Roop's assets. (If you find all of this complicated that's only because it is.)

All was ready for Roop to open a margin account at Waco. When you buy stock on margin you are basically using some of the brokerage firm's money to gamble – or, rather, to invest. For example, you buy 100 shares of Tesla at $300 a share for $30,000. But because you have assets and a good account, Waco lets you pay 50% now, or $15,000 for the shares. The other 50%, or $15,000, is on margin and is owed later. Now if Tesla goes to $400 a share you are golden. You sell the 100 shares for $40,000 and pay Waco their $15,000 back. And you get to keep the remaining $25,000 (less commissions). You only put up $15,000 on margin (instead of the full $30,000) and you made $5,000 more.

If it goes the other way you are not golden. Let's say Tesla drops to $100 a share. Your investment is worth $10,000 but you still owe Waco $15,000. They have the right to issue a margin call, meaning you owe the

Chapter Sixteen

$15,000 immediately. They can also sell all of your other stock holdings to pay off the margin call.

This is what happened to the Bad Boys. They used Roop to buy shares of Health Risk Management, Inc. (HRMI) on margin.

But then, as regulators do, NASDAQ halted trading of HRMI. The value of HRMI shares tanked and Waco issued a margin call on Roop's account. The entire Roop account was sold off but over $1.8 million was still owed to Waco.

Roop also owed money to Banco, the company controlled by Timmy's trust, and Roop defaulted on that obligation as well. Surprisingly, instead of trying to collect, Banco extended and expanded the line of credit to Roop. New money went in, but it wasn't used to pay back Waco. Instead, over $200,000 went to Timmy and Don as compensation, although the required W-2 forms were never issued. Roop's real estate assets were moved to a new entity, which was owned by other Bad Boy entities.

The Seventh Circuit Court, in reviewing the District Court's handling of the case, agreed with the District Court's finding that "Roop's assets were looted after it incurred its margin debt." It further stated that "... Roop may have maintained solvency until the HRMI stock it purchased on margin collapsed but that only marked the point at which Roop shareholders started raiding the company of its assets."

In their defense, the Bad Boys pointed out that there was a lack of evidence that Roop shareholders looted corporate coffers "to indulge a fancy lifestyle complete with extravagant houses, fancy cars, and other such luxuries." But as the court noted, "Waco didn't have to prove that Roop's money was drained to support fancy lifestyles. The district court found that Roop paid nearly $1.2 million to insiders or related entities... There was no error in the court's finding that Roop diverted its assets to its shareholders and related entities after incurring its debt to Waco."

The court stated: "Adhering to Roop's separate corporate existence would allow Roop's shareholders to leave Waco holding the bag for Roop's failed HRMI investment. The Roop shareholders used their web of corporations to avoid their responsibilities to Waco by ensuring that Roop would not have sufficient funds to pay their debts." Adhering to

Undercapitalization

Roop's corporate form would sanction an attempt by Roop's shareholders to set up "a flimsy organization to escape personal liability." The Bad Boys argued that "Waco knowingly assumed the same risk as Roop that the value of the stock would decline". But, as the Court noted, "Roop did not share any risk because Roop shuttled its assets elsewhere and a secured inside lender (Banco) encumbered whatever remained. As the district court found, Roop's shell status, the Banco-Roop line of credit, and its representations on the margin account created the false appearance of a company capable of covering potential losses on that account."

The court pierced the veil.

Now let's consider a less complicated case with fewer Bad Boys.

In re Artisan Custom Builders, LLC[35] involved an Iowa bankruptcy case. Johnny Novak did his general contracting work through Artisan Custom Builders, LLC ("ACB"). The business operated out of Johnny's basement and he was the sole everything – LLC member, contractor, estimator, cook and bottle washer.

Johnny contracted to build a $627,000 custom home in eastern Iowa on a bluff overlooking the Mississippi River. Johnny didn't finish the project on time and when he finally delivered the home to the owners there were numerous elements that weren't complete.

Johnny told the homeowners that the subcontractors (the plumbers, electricians and the like, also known as 'subs') had all been paid and their liens released. Subs will lien a property as security for payment of their services. When a lien is released, it means the sub has been paid and has no further claim of security against the property. Johnny told the homeowners that everything was clear.

But this wasn't true. The homeowners soon learned from the subs that Johnny hadn't paid them or if he had that the ACB checks had bounced.

The subs filed mechanics' liens against the homeowners' new house for over $130,000. The homeowners paid more than that, a total of $250,000, to complete the house and satisfy the liens.

Johnny's response was "Oops." He and his wife and ACB, LLC filed for bankruptcy to be done with it all. Some debts can be discharged in bankruptcy, but not all. Cases of fraud keen a court's attention. When

121

Chapter Sixteen

Johnny said the subs had been paid and the liens released that was a knowingly false representation. Johnny knew it wasn't true. False statements like that are considered fraud.

Bankruptcy courts need not discharge a fraud, which is a good policy. Think about it: What if everyone could lie and cheat and swindle and then go into bankruptcy and dismiss it all? That would not be a healthy or fair way to operate a legal system.

Of course, Johnny's attorney tried to defend him. That's what the attorney is paid to do. The argument was that the homeowners' contract was with ACB, LLC, and that Johnny was never personally responsible for any claims.

The court didn't buy it and pierced the veil, holding Johnny personally liable. ACB was undercapitalized for the business at hand and, as stated by the court "...the LLC is a mere sham which serves no legitimate business purpose." The homeowners' claims for over $240,000 were not discharged in bankruptcy and Johnny was held personally responsible for over $130,000.

So much for getting rid of everything in bankruptcy.

Undercapitalization played a large issue in this case. Johnny didn't have enough money into ACB to operate it properly. Furthermore, it appeared he didn't have any idea what an adequate level of capital would be. He just set up an LLC and went with it. But you can't operate a scofflaw entity and then expect it to protect you when things go awry. You need to have enough money into the business (which, granted, may be hard to calculate) to expect any sort of protection in return.

Let's consider one more complicated case where the veil was not pierced for undercapitalization.

Trade Winds Airlines, Inc. v. Soros[36] involved George Soros, the billionaire funder of progressive causes, as a defendant. Plaintiffs sometimes get the notion that suing billionaires will lead to quick and painless settlements, assuming that a billionaire won't want to be bothered. Billionaires, conversely, realize that settling cases will only lead to more litigation, assuming (perhaps rightly so) that by not fighting back they will only be more bothered by plaintiffs' attorneys in the future. As well,

Undercapitalization

some billionaires consider litigation sport. They own the franchise and their team is made up of lawyers ready for battle.

In this case, Trade Winds had a judgment against C-S Aviation Services, Inc. (C-S Aviation). Not being able to collect they sued George Soros and his partner Arnendu Chatterjee individually, seeking to pierce the C-S Aviation veil. C-S Aviation involved a myriad of management entities, special purpose vehicles and transactions that would keep a small law firm busy for years. Interestingly enough, when you got through the paper maze, it turned out Soros was never a shareholder, director or officer of C-S Aviation.

Soros and Chatterjee moved for summary judgment which, as discussed earlier, is a request for an early resolution of the case before proceeding to trial.

The parties agreed that Delaware law controlled the analysis of the veil piercing issue, since C-S Aviation was a Delaware corporation. The United States District Court for the Southern District of New York stated that, in order to pierce the corporate veil under Delaware law, Plaintiffs needed to show that:

> (1) C-S Aviation and Defendants operated as a single economic entity; and (2) an overall element of injustice or unfairness was present. The District Court noted that the relevant considerations for determining whether Defendants and C-S Aviation operated as a single economic entity included: (1) whether the corporation was adequately capitalized for the corporate undertaking; (2) whether the corporation was solvent; (3) whether dividends were paid; (4) whether corporate records were kept; (5) whether officers and directors functioned properly; (6) whether other corporate formalities were observed; (7) whether the dominant shareholder siphoned corporate funds; and (8) whether the corporation simply functioned as a façade for the dominant shareholder. The Court pointed out that some combination of these factors was required, because none alone was sufficient to disregard the corporate form, and that this analysis was used to determine whether there

Chapter Sixteen

had been a commingling of the operations of the entity and its owner. Plaintiffs argued, among other things, that C-S Aviation was undercapitalized. With regard to undercapitalization, the Court **assumed that C-S Aviation was undercapitalized**, but nevertheless set forth Plaintiffs' evidence of undercapitalization, as follows: (1) Chatterjee only paid $100 for 1,000 shares when establishing C-S Aviation; (2) Chatterjee also provided loans, noted on the general ledger, to help cover some of C-S Aviation's expenses; and (3) testimony from Soros suggested that he was more concerned with a separate aircraft leasing business making a profit than C-S Aviation being profitable.

The District Court concluded that, **even accepting Plaintiffs' above evidence of undercapitalization as adequate, undercapitalization alone was insufficient to pierce the corporate veil**. For this reason, among others, the Court granted Defendants' motion for summary judgment. Soros was not held personally liable, in yet another victory for billionaires everywhere.

Let's say you want to pierce the veil of a company you believe to be undercapitalized. What evidence do you need?

You could start by reviewing the company's financial statements and any independent audit reports. You can request those through the discovery process. Investment documents to and from shareholders would be good to see. You could depose (ask in person questions of) the chief financial officer and a CPA from the company's accounting firm. Was the company a going concern? Did it have the resources to properly operate?

Then start looking at capital flows. Was the company in a financial position to meet its obligations? Did money flow from the company to an alter ego defendant? Are those flows justified? Did the alter ego in turn pay any company expenses? Were the payment lines blurred? Did shareholders invest money into the company pursuant to their obligations? Did they invest any money at all?

It would also be helpful to know if the company is suitably capitalized and has an adequate level of assets for its specific business. An expert from

Undercapitalization

the industry you are dealing with can offer an opinion as to necessary funding levels for the business' operations.

Courts want to see evidence before piercing a veil. The more specific and relatable evidence you can provide, the better.

Proving up undercapitalization is not always easy. And know that your case is stronger if the undercapitalized claim is one of several other veil piercing factors.

Chapter Seventeen

Reverse Veil Piercing

You have a judgement against an individual. They have no assets but their entity does. Is it fair for that individual to be poor when their LLC or corporation is rich? Especially when their rich entity funds their rich lifestyle.

If you can pierce the corporate veil to get through to an individual why can't you reverse pierce to get through the poor individual to their rich entity? That seems fair and to more and more courts reverse piercing is a remedy for creditors.

Graphically, reverse piercing appears as follows:

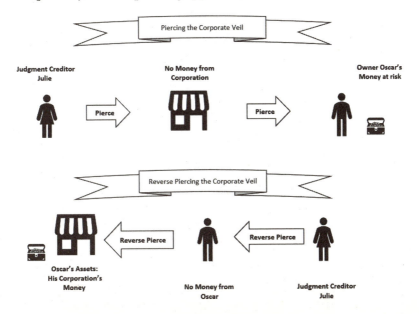

Chapter Seventeen

Can you reverse pierce the veil of a limited partnership? The Supreme Court of Virginia dealt with such a case.[37] Bobby Diamond was a business guy. He owned numerous businesses through numerous companies. Things were going well and he wanted to expand his aviation empire, known as Origin Air, LP. In 1993, he borrowed over $6 million from D.G. Trust for his company. The two promissory notes were personally guaranteed by Bobby and his wife Bonny.

Of course, the reason we're reviewing this case is because Bobby's companies ran into trouble and couldn't pay the money back. D.G. Trust went after Bobby and Bonny personally, since they had guaranteed the notes. In 1996, a Virginia Circuit Court entered a judgement against the Diamonds for the amount of the note plus interested owed to D.G. Trust.

For the next four years, D.G. Trust tried to collect on their judgment. They obtained a charging order against Bobby's companies, including Origin Air, LP. No payment. They obtained a garnishment order against Bobby's companies, including Tripass Holdings Group, Inc. No payment.

In 2000, D.G. Trust had had enough. They sued Bobby, Bonny and their eldest son Ron claiming that their entities were alter egos of them, one and the same, Clark Kent and Superman, and that they should be reverse pierced to pay up.

At trial that August, the evidence came out as to the two ways the Diamonds avoided paying D.G. Trust. First, Bobby directed monies from his companies to his wholly owned Tripass Holdings Group Inc. (THG). For a fee THG provided managerial and administrative services to all of Bobby's companies. But once D.G. Trust had its judgement Bobby directed another $2 million in over payments to THG, which then used that money to pay Bobby and Bonny's personal expenses.

Through this arrangement THG maintained the Diamond's $15,000 a month lifestyle. THG paid the mortgages on the Virginia and Martha's Vineyard houses, the Mercedes car payment, country club dues, college tuitions for the kids and even legal fees. Of note, D.G. Trust was not paid a penny.

Reverse Veil Piercing

Bobby testified that he received no salary from THG. Instead, he claimed the monies were just loan repayments. He had loaned money to the company in the past and was just repaying himself.

Unfortunately for him, his CPA testified under oath, and THG's own ledgers reflected, that the payments weren't loan repayments but rather distributions, the payment of profits. Having witnesses testify under penalty of perjury (meaning jail time for lying) does help a court get to the truth.

The second way the Diamonds avoided paying their debt was through Origin Air LP, which operated a large commercial airport. The LP's general partner was Redlands, Inc., which was owned by son Ron Diamond. Redlands owned the 2% general partnership interest and Bobby owned the 98% limited partnership interest. A few weeks after the D.G. Trust judgement was issued against him, Bobby transferred half, or 49%, of his limited partnership interests to his son Ron. Was this a fraudulent transfer?

Through this transaction Bobby purportedly surrendered control of Origin Air to Ron, who now owned 51%, his 2% Redlands general partnership interest and his newly received 49% limited partnership interest from Dad after the judgment. However, Bobby still managed all the day to day affairs at the airport. Bobby then directed Origin Air to distribute its profits to Ron, the majority owner. Once the money was in Ron's account, the son would then pay the personal expenses of his parents.

From the date of D.G. Trust's judgement at trial to the date of the reverse piercing trial, Ron received $4.3 million from Origin Air.

The court determined that Origin Air was the alter ego of Bobby Diamond and that the separate personalities between the two no longer existed. An appeal was filed with the Diamonds contending that one could pierce the corporate veil to get at a shareholder but that the court could not reverse pierce the shareholder to get at the company. The court swiftly rejected their argument, writing:

> "We conclude that there is no logical basis upon which to distinguish between a traditional veil piercing action and an outsider reverse

Chapter Seventeen

piercing action. In both instances, a claimant requests that a court disregard the normal protections accorded a corporate structure to prevent abuses of that structure."

Abuse of the structure. Significant abuse of the structure. This was the first time Virginia allowed a reverse piercing. But, as the facts indicated, when parties act in such a brazen fashion, courts will follow with appropriate remedies, even new and expanded ones. Of note, Delaware relied on Virginia's ruling to adopt reverse piercing in the 2021 *Manichaean Cap.* case.

Courts now allow a reverse piercing when the alter ego is not even an owner of the targeted corporation. Such was the case in *CFL Group vs. Folsom*,[38] decided by the Nevada Supreme Court in 2000. Willie and Carl were brothers involved in real estate. Carl owned 100% of CFL Group, Inc., a real brokerage firm. Willie had zero ownership in CFL. But he ran all of its operations.

Willie wrote all of the letters, negotiated all the contracts, hired and supervised all of CFL's brokers and agents and was listed as president and CEO of CFL. Willie sometimes even held himself out as CFL's primary owner, a misrepresentation with consequences.

The Folsom family had a $25,000 judgment against Willie as an individual. Willie had been held personally liable to them for a failed real estate transaction. The Folsoms had tried to collect from Willie for a number of years without success.

Then the Folsoms heard from a little birdie that a large Reno land holder had put over $25,000 into a local title company to pay CFL for future services. The Folsoms filed a motion to seize the deposited monies in the title company account.

A hearing was quickly held and the Folsoms argued that CFL was the alter ego of Willie. If one could go through CFL to reach Willie on an alter ego claim why couldn't they reach Willie through CFL on the same basis?

Reverse Veil Piercing

Willie argued that Nevada law did not allow for a reverse piercing. The court agreed—that it was time for a change. The Nevada Supreme Court wrote:

> We conclude that reverse piercing is not inconsistent with traditional piercing in its goal of preventing abuse of the corporate form. Indeed, "[i]t is particularly appropriate to apply the alter ego doctrine in 'reverse' when the controlling party uses the controlled entity to hide assets or secretly to conduct business to avoid the pre-existing liability of the controlling party.

Willie then argued: "But I don't own the company! I'm not a controlling party!" The Nevada Supreme Court saw it otherwise. They noted that Willie acted as the ultimate authority for all of CFL's dealings. They pointedly observed that Willie held himself out as the primary owner of CFL. (A word to the wise: If you hold yourself out as the owner—you may be held liable as one). The court found there was enough evidence to show a unity of interest and ownership between Willie and CFL.

The Folsom family collected from CFL in Nevada's first reverse piercing case. Many states now allow for reverse piercings. Where carefully designed business arrangements allow for an individual owing money to appear poor while their entity (whether directly owned or not) is very rich courts will follow the interests of justice and pierce the veil in reverse.

Chapter Eighteen

Wife vs. Husband.
Husband vs. Wife.

Canadians are some of the nicest people on earth. But when it comes to icing the divorce, they can hide assets with the world's best. Such was the case out of Ontario.[39] Bob McKenzie owned a business that manufactured beer bottling equipment. The beer profits were then distributed to a second corporation named Hoser Tech, which in Bob's eyes was owned only by Bob, and not by his soon to be ex-wife.

Under Canadian law, just as in the U.S., a corporation is considered a separate legal entity, standing alone in and of itself. The corporation can own its own assets separate from the shareholders of the entity.

Bob McKenzie decided that since he owned Hoser Tech all by himself he didn't need to report any of its holdings–investment accounts and real estate worth millions–to the court. Bob's wife made legal inquiries as to Hoser Tech, which Bob didn't bother to answer. He didn't file a Financial Statement on Hoser Tech's assets as was required in a divorce proceeding. For Bob, Hoser Tech's assets were 'untouchable' because they were protected and well–shielded behind 'his' corporate framework.

Ironically, Bob's attitude of what was 'his' lead to his fall. Because he treated the Hoser Tech assets as if they were his own, the court found that Hoser Tech was not a separate legal entity but rather was Bob's alter ego, an extension of himself. The court made the following key findings of fact:

1. Bob exercised complete control of Hoser Tech.
2. Bob used that control in a wrongful manner to protect himself from his wife's claims; and

Chapter Eighteen

3.   Bob's misconduct was the cause of his wife's financial losses.

The court pierced the veil of Hoser Tech. And in doing so the court boldly ordered the banks holding Hoser Tech assets to liquidate the accounts and transfer all the monies directly to the wife. Legal proceedings aren't always nice in Canada.

Sometimes ex-husbands sue ex-wives. The rancor continues.

Maryland's Court of Special Appeals dealt with such a case.[40] Isabel and Javier Palance were married real estate professionals and in August of 1961 they incorporated Palance Realty Inc. The business, which engaged in real estate sales and management activities, did well until the Palances experienced relationship difficulties. In September of 1972 the couple severed both marital and business ties.

A property settlement and stock redemption agreement was entered into whereby Isabel would buy Javier out of Palance Realty, Inc. over a period of seven years. The first payment of $29,000 was received by Javier, but no further annual payments were ever made.

Three months after she signed the settlement agreement Isabel incorporated Palance, Inc., which took over Palance Realty Inc's lucrative sales business. All the various sales locations changed their signage to the new name (with the old logo intact) and all the real estate agents switched their licenses into the new company's name. The same offices, office furniture and phone numbers were now used by the new Palance, Inc.

Isabel wasn't done. She then changed the name of Palance Realty, Inc. (the business that still owed Javier money) to Isabel Management, Inc., which continued on with only their less lucrative management activities. Isabel was able to continue the profitable sales operations through the new company, which she maintained had no obligation to Javier. She claimed the company that did owe him the money, the renamed Isabel Management, couldn't afford to pay anything. As the court stated: "The effect of all these corporate machinations is obvious."

As an attorney you always want your client to tell the truth. But sometimes...

Wife vs. Husband. Husband vs. Wife.

Isabel admitted in a deposition that when she signed the stock redemption agreement she had no intention of paying Javier for his Palance Realty, Inc. shares. She was bitter and brashly claimed the whole transaction was unfair, meaning she did not have to, nor would she, pay. That got the court's attention. "Where one person induces another to part with his money or property by means of a promise which she makes with the intention of not performing it, she is guilty of actionable fraud."

The fraudulent acts of a corporate agent (as Isabel was when she signed the stock redemption agreement as President of Palance Realty Inc.) are also not favored:

> In such a case not only is the corporation liable for such action, but the agents who engage in the conspiracy are personally liable for damages resulting from such a transaction. Agents of a corporation...cannot hide behind the corporate shield and say they were acting solely as the agents of the corporation.

Isabel was held personally responsible for the amount owed, interest and attorney's fees.

Shell games on the street where you try to guess which card the ball is under can be difficult. (At least I never guess right.) But sleight of hand tricks with corporations will not confuse many courts.

Chapter Nineteen

All in the Family Liability: Parent-Child, Sister Frankenstein

Parents frequently assert complete domination and control over their children which, especially when they are young, has seemed to work well since beginning of time. But when parent corporations assert such control over subsidiary children, the results are mixed.

Again, there is not a lot of consistency or clarity in this corner of law. As Judge Benjamin Cardozo, the esteemed New York jurist who served as an Associate Justice on the US Supreme Court, wrote in a 1926 opinion:

> The whole problem of the relation between parent and subsidiary corporations is one that is still enveloped in the mists of metaphor. Metaphors in law are to be carefully watched, for starting as devices to liberate thoughts, they end often by enslaving it.

In an Oklahoma Supreme Court case[41] the Patterson family sued a local hospital on a wrongful death matter. They also sued the subsidiary hospital's much larger parent corporation, which operated a nationwide chain of hospitals. The Pattersons argued that the parent was also responsible for their subsidiary (or 'sub') when it came to damages. The parent corporation wanted no part of their subsidiary's liability and fought the case to Oklahoma's highest court.

The Oklahoma Supreme Court laid out their rules forthrightly:

> The question whether an allegedly dominate corporation may be held liable for a subservient entity's tort hinges primarily on control. Factors which may be considered at trial include whether

137

Chapter Nineteen

1) the parent corporation owns all or most of the subsidiary's stock, 2) the corporations have common directors or officers, 3) the parent provides financing to its subsidiary, 4) the dominant corporation subscribes to all the other's stock, 5) the subordinate corporation is grossly undercapitalized, 6) the parent pays the salaries, expenses or losses of the subsidiary, 7) almost all of the subsidiary's business is with the parent or the assets of the former were conveyed from the latter, 8) the parent refers to its subsidiary as division or department, 9) the subsidiary's officers or directors follow directions from the parent corporation, and 10) legal formalities for keeping the entities separate and independent are observed.

When the court reviewed all the factors, including the parent owning 100% of their sub, common management and the parents guaranteeing all of the subs' obligations, they found that the sub was a mere instrumentality of the parent and remanded the case to the lower court for further proceeding.

Parents, in life and in the law, can be held responsible for their children. Family liability also extends to sister entities. In a New York case[42] the Redfield family owed two companies, Baxter and Fillmore, which borrowed money from plaintiffs based upon false representations that the money would be used for working capital purposes. Instead, as the court found, the Redfield:

> Defendants used the companies' money as a personal checking account for their own use and expenses such as their mother's plastic surgery, their monthly household bills and parking tickets; that the Redfield's ran the companies without regard for corporate and bookkeeping formalities; that Baxter and Fillmore were undercapitalized; and that the commingling of corporate and personal funds was a regular and continuous practice.

The court also noted that the two sister entities had an overlap in ownership, officers and directors, used common office space and telephone numbers without distinction and were not treated as independent profit centers. Veil piercing both sister entities was easily justified, especially in light of mom's plastic surgery. Facts like that have a way of forever sticking out.

The familial relationship of sister companies allow some courts to create new responsibilities. In such cases, the court mashes the sister companies together to create one new responsible entity. This is the third major approach to veil piercing: The Single Enterprise Theory. Or the Sister Frankenstein theory whereby various parts are brought together into one new whole body. As a California court famously stated in *Las Palmas*[43]:

> Generally, alter ego liability is reserved for the parent-subsidiary relationship. However, under the single-enterprise rule, liability can be found between sister companies. The theory has been described as follows: "In effect what happens is that the court, for sufficient reasons, has determined that though there are two or more personalities, there is but one enterprise; and that this enterprise has been so handled that it should respond, as a whole, for the debts of certain component elements of it. The court thus has constructed for purposes of imposing liability *an entity unknown to any secretary of state comprising assets and liabilities of two or more legal personalities*; endowed that entity with the assets of both, and charged it with the liabilities of one or both. (Emphasis added)

It's alive!

In the *Las Palmas* case the Court noted that each sister was an instrumentality or mirror conduit of the other. The unity of interest and ownership of each sister company was so close "that the separation of the two corporations had in effect ceased." As a result, the Single Enterprise rule takes the two sisters and merges them together as conjoined twins to make one new single responsible entity.

But what if you don't want your entities mashed together as one? You have perfectly legitimate reasons for having a whole Thanksgiving dinner gathering of independent parents, children, brothers and sisters and

Chapter Nineteen

they've better sit and stay in their own seats and not be held responsible for each other. Fear not. There are ways to keep all of your corporations, LLCs and other entities separated and apart and not mixed together. The strategies are discussed in Chapter 24.

But first, what if you just want to end it all?

Chapter Twenty

Dissolve and Run?

Roger Piston and Albert Dunham operated on the edge. Some cursed their lawyering. Others, as we shall see, actively oppose lawyers who lower the standards of the profession. And by lowering we mean going so low as to misuse the system to shake people down on porn claims.

Piston and Dunham set up 'law firms' in various states to misuse subpoena powers. A court ordered subpoena can allow for the finding of all sorts of private and confidential information, which, for some attorneys, including these two, can be used for improper purposes.

In the Minnesota case[44] the court described Piston and Dunham's activities in other states. In some jurisdictions they brought copyright claims directly against John Doe defendants. (When you don't know the name of the supposed wrongdoer you can file your complaint against 'John Doe' and hopefully through later discovery ascertain the real name and replace 'John Doe' with the real person.) Once they learned the identities of who was misusing X-rated copyrighted material, the attorneys would then threaten to expose and embarrass the voyeur unless a $3,400 settlement was paid. It was a very crass and lucrative shakedown.

In other states, Piston and Dunham brought a computer hacking claim against a single, passive defendant and next sought discovery of the many Internet subscribers alleged to have conspired with the defendant. Then, with all those names, they would shake down innocents with the claim of downloading X-rated movies. Of course, many people would prefer to pay several thousands of dollars to avoid the embarrassment of such a tawdry

Chapter Twenty

claim. (Although, now that 75% of Americans watch porn on their cell phones at least once a month, perhaps the racket has lost its 'morality.')

Still, courts do not like lawyers misusing subpoena powers to shake down innocents or, even in the case of downloading copyrighted porn, not so innocents.

The Minnesota case was a set up. In September 2012, Ray Holly, an Oregon resident, received a letter from Compre Law Firm, LLC (one of Piston and Dunham's firms) alleging he had downloaded porn from the internet in violation of their client Mango's rights. The penalty was $3,400. Holly called the law firm and said he couldn't possibly pay that amount. Mike, a lawyer at the firm, offered an alternative settlement. Holly would agree to be sued by Mango. Then Compre would ask for, and Holly would provide, his bit-torrent log. Mike provided Holly with the name of another Minnesota attorney who would represent him on a pro bono (free) basis. Holly, it was agreed, would not be held responsible in the case.

Compre Law then sued Holly in Minnesota, alleging, without much detail, that Holly engaged in a civil conspiracy with others to access copyrighted material. The complaint was signed by Albert Dunham, the attorney with the Compre Law Firm, LLC. Ten days later, Compre filed an unopposed discovery motion for a court order to obtain subpoenas against more than 300 internet service providers (ISPs) in order to discover Holly's alleged co-conspirators. Of course, the motion was unopposed because Holly was in their pocket. Compre Law requested many thousands of names, email and physical addresses, phone numbers and media access control addresses. With this information Piston and Dunham would gain a bonanza list of extortion victims.

The court held a hearing on October 31, 2012 to review the request. Neither defendant Holly nor his pro bono attorney showed up (which was conveniently prearranged) to oppose the motion. The court, perhaps smelling a rat, denied the motion concluding that Mango and Compre "had not demonstrated that the personally identifying information possessed by over 300 ISPs...is relevant and material to this matter."

Dissolve and Run?

A week later Compre filed an 'emergency renewed unopposed discovery motion for authorizing order' (a clunky and rookie request) seeking subpoenas against 17 ISPs. Compre asserted that "these specific ISPs unquestionably possess information connected to the issues in this litigation." They provided no evidence for this assertion. The court, perhaps forcing the issue, granted the motion but allowed the targeted ISPs 30 days to file motions to quash the subpoenas.

At this time, ISPs were getting fed up with phony subpoena requests from attorneys the likes of Piston and Dunham. The ISPs fought back.

At a January 25, 2013 hearing the ISPs asserted that "the litigation was being pursued for the improper purpose of using third-party discovery to obtain names of Internet subscribers from whom settlements could be extorted." In support they provided an affidavit from Holly on how he'd been set up from Oregon to be the nominal and un-opposing defendant in the Mango case and that no discovery had been requested of him. The ISPs also argued that Mango had never qualified to do business in Minnesota and thus did not have authority to sue in Minnesota courts. (As we discussed in Chapter 10, this is always a great argument to make.)

Perhaps feeling the heat, and before the court ruled on the motion to quash, Mango and Compre moved to dismiss the case. On the same day the ISPs filed a motion seeking to recover attorney's fees for having to defend themselves against Mango's subpoena fishing expedition. An Order to Show Cause (OSC) hearing was set for April 23rd requiring Mango, Dunham and Compre Law to personally appear and show the court why they shouldn't be required "to pay the reasonable attorney's fees and costs incurred by the non-parties to this action." The ISPs wanted their money back.

As the court wrote in our slightly amended names changed version (but with the court's emphasizing Dunham's use of the word I):

> Attorney Dunham appeared at the April 23 hearing, without any corporate representative attending for Mango. Dunham stated: "My understanding, and **I** guess it was incorrect is that as an agent as an attorney for Mango that **I** could represent them in

Chapter Twenty

this matter as certainly **I've** done throughout of the entirety of the case." The district court pressed Dunham for a reason why no evidence had been presented regarding Mango's structure or its business:

Why don't **I** have anything from them? **I** mean why don't **I** have any documents since you know that they're alleging it's fraudulent? If **I** agree that it's fraudulent then **I** could, **I** would have a basis to Order you to pay attorney's fees so because **I'm** saying it looks like you're doing this fraud on the Court. So if you want to show **me** that you're not doing a fraud on the Court, then why wouldn't you say Your Honor, this is wholly unjust, how dare they say these things? Look here's my affidavit from the President and CEO of Mango LLC. This is the nature of the business that we do. This is how we found out about what Mr. Holly was doing. Why don't **I** have anything like that? ... Why don't **I** have an affidavit from someone from Mango LLC other than you?

In responding to the district court's concerns about fraud, Dunham asserted for the first time at the OSC hearing that the action was filed in Minnesota because it was convenient to Piston and Dunham as counsel. Dunham also conceded that Mango still had not filed a certificate of authority pursuant to *Minn. Stat. § 322B.94* but argued that Mango was not doing business in Minnesota and thus the statute did not apply. Dunham also conceded that no discovery had been sought from Holly but again asserted that the third-party discovery was of primary importance. Dunham also denied any connection between the communications that Holly had with "Mike" or "Michael" at Compre Law and this action, asserting, "**I** made no offer, **I** made no deal."

The court (as courts are good at doing) saw through it all and ordered Mango, Dunham and Compre to jointly and severally (meaning each was responsible for the full amount and the ISPs could go after whoever they wanted for it) pay $64,000 to the ISP's attorneys within 30 days. The

Dissolve and Run?

Court also required Dunham and Compre to post a $10,000 bond in any future litigation on behalf of entities that must be qualified to do business in Minnesota.

The Court then made two other distinct findings. They found that Dunham, based on his words and actions, lacked any credibility, stating that any of his "declarations and testimony offered is discredited with this Court." And they found that Dunham and the Compre Law Firm LLC "acted in bad faith and without a basis in law and fact to initiate this action."

It is here that attorney Roger Piston, the owner of Compre Law, comes to the forefront. Two weeks after the hearing on the motion to quash the subpoenas, he transferred $65,000 from Compre to another law firm he owned. Then, one week after the OSC hearing, he transferred $80,000 from Compre to his personal account. And finally, two weeks after the court granted sanctions against Compre, Piston dissolved Compre. As part of the dissolution, Piston certified that Compre had no debts or pending proceedings against it. As Elvis sang so succinctly: That was just a lie.

Minnesota courts consider two prongs when piercing the veil: 1) the individual and corporation relationship and 2) the corporation and veil-piercer relationship.

On the first test the court found that Piston used Compre for personal purposes, insufficiently funded and intentionally defunded the entity and kept no corporate records. Moreover, Compre never followed standard law firm requirements of maintaining malpractice insurance and a client trust account.

The second test was also met. The court held it would be fundamentally unfair if they didn't pierce the veil and hold Piston personally responsible. Piston's actions brought all of this upon himself. He took affirmative steps to prevent the ISPs from collecting by transferring money out of and then dissolving Compre Law Firm, LLC before any claims were paid. A professional LLC will not protect the professional who brings bad faith litigation into court and then tries to hide from the consequences.

The ISPs achieved justice.

Chapter Twenty

Dissolving your entity and running away has not worked well in other cases either. In the Miami Tru-Color case[45] their subsidiary, named Tru-Color, breached a lease by simply stopping payments. The landlord sought to pierce the subsidiary's veil to hold the parent company liable. The lower court weighed the evidence which showed:

> ...the absence of the formalities and paraphernalia of corporate existence of Tru-Color; its inadequate capitalization; an overlap in ownership, officers, directors and personnel; common addresses and telephone numbers; payments of Tru-Color's debts by Miami Tru-Color; and use by Miami Tru- Color of Tru-Color's property. Further, funds were shifted back and forth to the extent that Tru-Color was insolvent at the time the breach occurred.

The appellate court held: "That the lower court properly pierced the corporate veil and properly held that dissolution did not affect liability occurring prior to dissolution."

However, in some cases dissolution can get you beyond responsibility for a claim. A key component is the statute of limitations, which is the time period in which a claim must be filed.

Statute of limitations were first brought forth by the Byzantine Roman emperor Justinian in 529 A.D. Justinian liked order, and decades long blood feuds where grandsons fought to avenge their grandfathers' wrongings upset that order. So, under the Empire's law and virtually all legal systems since, you had to assert your claim within a certain time period, sometimes one year, sometimes ten years depending on the claim. If you missed the time period, your claim could not be heard. It was null and void. This rule did end a number of blood feuds.

In the Purdom case[46] out of Illinois the issue was could the plaintiffs collect from the officers and directors of a dissolved corporation. Importantly, the claim against the corporation arose before it became inactive.

Plaintiff Ethyl Purdom fell while she was walking on a parking lot owned by The Campbell Group, Inc. ("Campbell"). She filed a negligence action against Campbell, seeking to recover damages from the corporation

146

Dissolve and Run?

for the injuries she allegedly suffered as a result of the fall. Her husband, Greg Purdom, also sought damages for loss of consortium (or a loss of sexual intimacies). Meanwhile, the Illinois Secretary of State involuntarily dissolved Campbell for its failure to file a report and pay its taxes. The trial court entered a default judgment against Campbell. After conducting a prove-up to determine plaintiffs' damages, the trial court entered a judgment against the company awarding Ethyl Purdom $1 million in damages and Greg Purdom $100,000 in damages. Plaintiffs initiated collection proceedings against Campbell, but they were unsuccessful because Campbell was insolvent.

The Plaintiffs and their attorneys wanted payment. They next went after Campbell's directors and shareholders individually, alleging that the defendants disregarded the corporate form and that Campbell was a mere facade for the operation of its shareholders. They sought to pierce Campbell's corporate veil and to collect their judgment in the underlying litigation from the defendants personally.

What followed was an expensive back and forth procedural battle fought in various counts though various appeals. At issue was which statute of limitations period applied: The two year statute for personal injury claims or the five year statute, which provided that dissolution of a corporation did not extinguish a piercing claim against individuals for five years after the dissolution. After much costly wrangling (fueled part by the attorneys, who were entitled to a share of the $1.1 million judgment) the Illinois Court of Appeals held that the five year rule applied. Because the Purdoms had filed within the statutory period, a piercing action against the directors and shareholders was allowed. But if the Purdoms had waited too long the dissolution would act to bar their claims. You can dissolve and run under the right circumstances.

Many states allow for existing claims against dissolved entities to be time barred. Wyoming law, for example, allows a dissolved LLC to publish notice which shall:

> 1) Be published at least once in a newspaper of general circulation in the county in this state in which the dissolved limited liability

Chapter Twenty

company's principal office is located or, if it has none in this state, in the county in which the company's designated office is or was last located;

2) Describe the information required to be contained in a claim and provide a mailing address to which the claim is to be sent; and

3) State that a claim against the company is barred unless an action to enforce the claim is commenced within three (3) years after the publication of the notice.

If the notice is properly handled the claimant has three (3) years to file a lawsuit against the dissolved entity. After that, the claimant has no further rights to assert a claim.

Nevada takes a different approach as found in NRS 78.585(1):

The dissolution of a corporation does not impair any remedy or cause of action available to or against it or its directors, officers or stockholders commenced within 2 years after the date of the dissolution with respect to any remedy or cause of action in which the plaintiff learns, or in the exercise of reasonable diligence should have learned of, the underlying facts on or before the date of dissolution, or within 3 years after the date of dissolution with respect to any other remedy or cause of action. Any such remedy or cause of action not commenced within the applicable period is barred. The corporation continues as a body corporate for the purpose of prosecuting and defending suits, actions, proceedings and claims of any kind or character by or against it and of enabling it gradually to settle and close its business, to collect its assets, to collect money and other property among the stockholders, after paying or adequately act to wind up and liquidate its business and affairs, but not for the purpose of continuing the business for which it was established.

So in Nevada, claims against the entity (and almost more importantly, against the directors, officers and stockholders) must be filed within 2 years on known claims and 3 years on unknown claims.

Dissolve and Run?

Next door in California, a claimant, as a general rule, must file their action within four years after the effective date of a California dissolution or be time barred.

In Florida the statute of limitations is generally four years after the filing of notice whereas in New York it is not less than six months after the first publication of notice of dissolution. In Ohio it is not less than sixty days after notice is provided and Colorado is five years after notice. So in four large states we have statutes of limitations ranging from sixty days and six months, to four years and five years. Know that the rules vary from state to state. We have included the statutory language for Florida, New York, Ohio and Colorado in Appendix C for your use and understanding.

Dissolution isn't an abrupt termination. It is more like hospice, whereby the entity is prepared to be wound up and liquidated without any unnecessary or prolonging delays. And to further the metaphor into estate planning, both the entity's documents and the state's rules come into play. Just as individuals have living trusts and wills to set forth their final wishes, so do LLCs have Operating Agreements and corporations have bylaws governing their endings. But if an individual passes intestate (without a will) or an entity's documents are silent on winding up, the state's rules in both scenarios will be utilized as a backup or default. While the state rules aren't really evil, most individuals and entities would rather dictate their own course. Make sure you know your ending at the beginning.

So a dissolved entity exists not for conducting whatever business it did before but for the purpose of winding things up.

In most cases dissolution begins with a triggering event. When that event occurs, the corporate documents may require the entity to start winding up. For example, an Operating Agreement may set forth that the LLC shall hold a specific piece of real estate and that when that real estate is sold – a triggering event – the LLC must be dissolved and terminated.

Some LLC state regulations also provide for more than just voluntary dissolution by the owners. LLCs that fail to follow various compliance requirements (like paying the state's annual fee) may be administratively

Chapter Twenty

dissolved. An LLC that gets into deep trouble such as committing criminal or willful civil bad acts may be judicially dissolved in state court.

In the voluntary dissolution the owners of the LLC or corporation take a vote to approve dissolution. It is important to read your Operating Agreement or bylaws to know what percentage is required in favor of it and whether meetings, notice and any other formalities are required.

If your Operating Agreement or bylaws don't set forth such requirements then your state's default rules apply, some of which may require a unanimous vote to dissolve. The larger the pool of owners you have in any one entity the more risk you have that one spiteful person won't vote 'yes' on anything. You may want to assert your own percentage (66% or 75%, for example) rather than default to a state rule requiring 100% approval.

Almost all states require the filing of Articles of Dissolution, which provides notice to your state's Secretary of State (and the world) that you are in the process of winding up. This filing is an easy first step. (As an example, Corporate Direct charges $295 for the filing, plus applicable state filing fees.)

The winding up steps are more involved. While each entity in each state will have its own requirements, as a general rule the following tasks will need to be taken care of:

1. Withdrawing from states where the entity was registered as a foreign entity
2. Canceling business licenses and permits
3. Notifying creditors of the entity's dissolution
4. Paying those creditors
5. Closing any bank or other financial accounts; and
6. Filing final tax returns and reports

Paying those taxes is key. Most states will not allow a termination unless all the state taxes are paid. Some may require a tax clearance certificate to be filed before allowing a termination. Some states may require Articles of Termination, sometimes called Articles of Cancellation, to be filed stating that all debts and liabilities have been paid.

Dissolve and Run?

When all the winding up is wound up, any remaining assets may be distributed to the owners. Typically, the bank account is closed after this final step. Check your Operating Agreement or bylaws for any special rules on final distributions.

We started the chapter with those who improperly dissolved and ran. But know that planning an orderly dissolution, and extinguishing any lingering claims over time, is a good strategy. So is the alternative of keeping the corporation alive until the regular statute of limitation periods have run.

Chapter Twenty-One

The Government Piercith

As with any of us, the government likes to be paid. And they like to promptly receive those payroll taxes that employers withhold from their employees. The IRS considers that their money, which is needed to fund Uncle Sam's massive Social Security obligations which have been promised but, to read the government's own reports, may never be fully satisfied.

Employers who deduct payroll taxes but, because they need the money elsewhere in the business, don't forward them on to the IRS receive special attention. Broad, negative and piercing attention.

The IRS will pierce the corporate veil and hold individuals personally liable for unpaid payroll taxes. The question becomes who is a 'reasonable person' in the eyes of the IRS and thus subject to personal liability. A worker on the line is clearly not responsible. Neither is your receptionist. But a president who delegates financial activities and authority to others can certainly be personally liable for someone else's failure to transmit payroll taxes to the government.

Consider the following case[47]. Cooper and Barry ran an oil drilling company in Louisiana. Cooper, a CPA by training, handled the financial matters and Barry dealt with the day to day of oil rigs and drilling jobs. Barry relied on Cooper's oral assurances that all was fine in their financial house. Until one day it wasn't. When Barry finally confronted Cooper, it was learned that over $600,000 in withheld payroll taxes had not been forwarded to the IRS. Cooper had put it to other uses within the company.

Chapter Twenty-One

The IRS sued both Cooper and Barry personally for the money. Cooper had a summary judgment entered against him but since he didn't have any money the IRS continued against Barry as a second responsible person.

At trial the jury did not agree with the IRS's case. They found that Cooper 'hid everything from everybody else' and 'was totally in control'. They could not characterize Barry as a responsible person and thus did not find him personally liable for the $600,000.

The IRS didn't like the verdict and appealed. The next court noted a list of factors bearing upon the issue of responsibility, which included whether a person: (1) has power to compel or prohibit the allocation of funds; (2) has authority to sign checks: (3) had authority to make decisions as to disbursement of funds and payment of creditors; (4) was an officer or director of the corporation; (5) had control over the company's payroll; (6) prepared and signed payroll tax returns; (7) actively participated in the day-to-day management of the corporation; and/or (8) hired and fired employees.

The court found enough factors present in the case to hold Barry personally liable as a responsible person. But not all courts see the issue so broadly. In *Godfrey v. U.S.*,[48] the court found that in the absence of any evidence that the chairman of the board had or exercised control of the collection, accounting for, and payment over taxes, he could not be held liable for the failure to pay withholding taxes.

Still, you don't want to be held personally liable for company tax obligations. Make certain that whoever is responsible for their payment is actually sending in the checks to the IRS. You don't want to be on the hook as secondary responsible party.

The government will also pierce the veil in environmental cases.

CERCLA

The Comprehensive Environment Response Compensation and Liability Act of 1980 (sometimes called "CERCLA" or "Superfund") is aimed at

The Government Piercith

cleaning up the environment. This noble goal can get complicated very quickly. As an example, between 1986 and 1989 the insurance industry spent $1.3 billion on Superfund claims, of which $1 billion went to attorneys. To be clear, legal fees do not clean up the environment.

Courts have had a difficult time, perhaps due to the many billions spend on litigation, wrestling with the following issues:

1. Should parent companies be held liable for their subsidiary's acts?
2. Should officers, directors and shareholders be personally liable for the faults of their business?
3. Should successor companies be held liable for acts of their predecessors?

As one commentator has stated: "Efforts to predict when courts will or will not impose liability in a corporate context under CERCLA results in little more than a roll of the dice."

It is important to know that some courts have held parents liable for their subsidiaries and individuals liable for their company's acts. One case of such liability is discussed as the second badge of fraud in Appendix A. Overall, when you are dealing with anything related to environmental liabilities you must be very cautious. Stay out of court, if possible, for you will never be certain if your corporate protections will be respected.

ERISA

Like payroll tax withholding, paying money (or not) into private retirement plans can also result in individual liability.

The Employee Retirement Income Security Act of 1974 (ERISA) governs pension and retirement plans. Many of the best plans are negotiated by unions to both benefit their members and to prove the union's organizational value to their members. As in: "Yeah, you're paying us monthly dues but look what you're getting." And when pension obligations aren't met the union guys sue, to protect their members and to further justify their dues.

Chapter Twenty-One

A classic case in this area would be black-hearted directors converting their workers' pension monies for their own personal use. You can imagine them in the board room laughing with the glee as they misuse the retirement monies of others. You easily could pierce the veil that scenario, and you could also sue the directors directly for fraud. Cases have been brought directly against management for such frauds.

But we don't have many reported piercing cases. (Perhaps many such cases settle.) The meager record shows unions suing companies that just couldn't make the payments. But there's no black- hearted alter ego controlling individual. Instead, the companies followed all the corporate formalities but just couldn't meet their obligations. Management tried to make it but couldn't. Are the individual officers and directors then at fault? As one court noted, if Congress wanted to hold individuals personally responsible for unpaid pension contributions they would have done so.

Of course, if you obligate your company to fund a retirement plan you should make the payments. At the same time, you should be adhering to all the corporate formalities just in case things don't work out.

Chapter Twenty-Two

Piercing Around the World

Limited liability entities are allowed in free market economies around the world. When it comes to piercing these entities, however, the rules are all over the map.

United Kingdom

Lifting the corporate veil, as it is more politely known in the UK, does not occur with great frequency. Such a remedy is only granted if wrongdoing is present. In most cases, creditors are trying to recover losses for a corporation that has become insolvent. The goal is to find evidence that an owner of the failed company engaged in wrongful conduct. With the right case involving the right facts you may lift the veil.

Commonwealth Countries

Australia, New Zealand and other commonwealth countries inherited many of their statutory and judicial precedents from the UK. Accordingly, like the UK, they are reluctant to pierce the veil unless an injustice of some kind exists and, in tort cases, where there also exists prior intent to commit an act of fraud or injustice. Courts in New Zealand will pierce on occasion, but one scholar argues that "it is difficult to... rationalize" these cases.

Chapter Twenty-Two

Canada is a commonwealth exception. Maple Leaf Courts have been more willing to pierce the veil, just like their noisy neighbors to the south. As a rule, the courts in Canada must find three conditions to justify piercing: (1) the company must be an authorized agent of its controllers or of its corporate or human owners; (2) it must be demonstrated that the company is a "mere façade"; and (3) the piercing is necessary to give effect to a statute, contract, or other legally binding document.

France

Although the French legal system differs substantially from the U.S. system, France's laws and decisions regarding veil piercing are similar to their Yorktown allies. When shareholders fail to respect corporate separateness and engage in fraud or injustice, the French courts may hold shareholders personally liable. France does not recognize one-member limited liability companies. The minimum number of owners is two. France uses national statutes and equitable doctrines from case law to decide whether to pierce the veil. When companies do not meet national Bankruptcy Statute requirements, creditors can often obtain a ruling to disregard corporate separateness, thus holding the shareholders liable for the debts. Generally, shareholders or parent corporations that play a managerial role and engage in fraud or mismanagement are held responsible, as opposed to absentee shareholders who do not manage the company. Ownership itself is not grounds for piercing in parent corporation cases. It must be shown that the parent company played a key role in causing the financial collapse of the company.

Creditors may also pierce through on one of three different equitable doctrines. The first is a showing that the debtor company was fictitious, or a sham, created to defraud someone else out of money. The second involves the commingling of assets, wherein there is no real distinction between the company and its owners. The third is the doctrine of the appearance of corporate groups. This doctrine is similar to the U.S. doctrine of enterprise liability whereby a parent and subsidiary or sister companies mislead the victim as to the role that each is playing.

Germany

German law on veil piercing tracks the law in the United States closely, although the two legal systems have different histories. The doctrine of piercing in Germany is called 'Durchgriffshaftung', the key syllable being 'shaft,' as German courts will freely pierce for the benefit of those who have been shafted. And the probability of piercing increases as firm size decreases, when corporate formalities are not observed, and when a closely held firm is dominated by a single shareholder.

Like the United States, Germany has two types of corporate entities. One is similar to the U.S. public corporation and the other is a private, closely held limited liability company, which can have as few as one owner. The U.S. LLC is derived from this second German entity, the GmBH.

Several doctrines are used to pierce the corporate veil in Germany. One approach involves looking at factors such as commingling of assets, whether the parties adhered to corporate formalities, undercapitalization and domination by an individual or parent corporation. Interestingly, gathering evidence of commingling is done by the court, not the plaintiff. As in the United States, undercapitalization by itself is not grounds for piercing, but it is one factor. German law requires higher minimum capital levels than the U.S. law.

Enterprise liability may be available when schemes involve "commingling of funds and material undercapitalization of the subsidiary." In contrast to American jurisprudence, a finding of fraud or wrongdoing is not necessary to pierce when it can be shown that a parent corporation or other legal entity exercised domination over the debtor company. In such cases the controlling entity is liable straight away for the debts of the subsidiary firm.

Chapter Twenty-Two

Latin American Countries

Most Central and South American countries allow creditors and tort plaintiffs to pierce the veil in cases of fraud or gross negligence, with Argentina and Mexico on either end of the spectrum.

Argentina was the first Latin American nation to bring forth regulatory veil piercing in 1983 with a new statutory rule (Law 22.903). This law stipulated that "the liabilities of a corporation used to seek a purpose beyond the corporate goals, as a mere instrument to defraud the law, the public policy or the good faith, or to frustrate rights of a third person, will be imputed directly to its shareholders or to the controlling persons who facilitated such activities." Three elements generally are necessary to trigger a veil piercing: (1) corporate control; (2) fraud or misconduct; and (3) damage or unfair loss to third parties.

Several years ago, I was speaking at a Robert Kiyosaki event in Buenos Aires. I mentioned piercing the veil in my talk and wondered how prevalent it was Argentina. Afterwards, a very professional female attorney came up to me and said that the courts in Argentina pierced the veil all the time. Readers are forewarned.

Mexico is at the other end, allowing readers to relax. Mexican courts have never embraced the veil piercing concept, and many analysts believe the current law falls far short of protecting creditors.

Under the 1934 Mexican General Law of Corporations (LGSM), a corporation must consist of at least two parties and the legal system treats the corporation as a contract among investors seeking to achieve a common goal. As in the United States and other countries, shareholders are only responsible for debts up to the amount of their investments. The drafters of the LGSM recognized that shareholders have incentives to abuse limited liability by removing assets at the expense of creditors, so they created three legal protections: (1) minimum capitalization requirements; (2) statutory reserves; and (3) dividend restrictions. And yet, the level of proof involved is so difficult to reach that it has been reported that no Mexican court has ever pierced a corporate veil.

Piercing Around the World

Chile's law on piercing is unique. It is designed to allow workers to collect on wages owed. Let's say there is a big box retailer with stores up and down Chile known as Chil Mart. Each separate store is its own corporation. When a worker tries to collect on wages due from the Antofagasta store in the north the manager says: "So sorry. Our store is broke." The worker responds: "But this is Chil Mart, the biggest store in Chile. How can you be broke?" The law in Chile allows the worker to blow past the local store corporation and reach the rich corporate parent.

China

Piercing the corporate veil in China is a relatively new development, even though limited liability has certainly protected and will continue to protect Communist Party members who operate businesses. The once promising movement toward privatizing some areas of the economy led the Chinese to adopt some aspects of American law. In general, China pierces the veil more often than the United States and other countries. One theory is that the Chinese legal system still distrusts the idea that individuals can pursue profits for the benefit of all – a principle that remains a cornerstone for other modern economies.

The National People's Congress of the People's Republic of China (PRC) in 2005 enacted the New Company Law statute, which governs limited liability companies and also single-member owners. Initially, the law requires LLCs with one or two members to have a minimum level of capitalization, but these requirements were eliminated for the most newly created LLCs.

There are four general conditions under which a company's veil may be pierced in China.

The first involves a controlled (subsidiary) company. The courts may pierce when the financing and management are so closely connected to the parent company that the subsidiary does not have any independent decision-making authority and then it enters into a transaction that is beneficial to the parent company but detrimental to a third party.

Chapter Twenty-Two

Similar to the first condition, the second condition for piercing exists when the company is not treated by its owners as a separate entity, or the standard alter ego doctrine.

The third condition is undercapitalization. If shareholders fail to sufficiently capitalize a company and it then defaults on debts, a court can hold the shareholders responsible for repaying the debt.

The fourth condition is breach of duty during liquidation. The court may pierce the veil if the shareholders (a) fail to establish and commence a liquidation within the statutory time limits; (b) delay paying obligations during the liquidation; and (c) engage in fraud or deception with respect to the dissolution process. As in many other countries, there is no complete certainty as to when a veil will or will not be pierced in China.

Japan

Business law in Japan has had a substantial influence on the laws in South Korea and Taiwan, but Japan, interestingly, owes much of its law to the Germans. Part of this stems from the fact that the Japanese government in 1881 commissioned German legal scholar Hermann Roseler to draft a new commercial code. However, at the end of World War II, another commercial code was developed that drew heavily on the 1933 Illinois Business Corporation Act. So Japan, wisely again, drew from German and American influences.

Japan extends limited liability to stock companies but allows courts to disregard the corporate veil in some cases. The Japanese Supreme Court in 1969 declared that a court may pierce the veil when a company is a sham or when the company was created or used to avoid "contractual duties or application of the law." The court's decision was based on a case in which the owner of an electrical appliance store organized the corporation to evade taxes. As is true around the world, governments will pierce the veil to get paid.

Control is a necessary condition for piercing under this approach, but, as is the case in most other countries, not the only one. The courts also

Piercing Around the World

look for abusive activities, including inadequate capitalization, avoidance of debt, unfair labor practices and violations of non-compete agreements.

As is the case in the United States, where all 50 states have different piercing standards, across the globe standards also vary greatly. Piercing the corporate veil has never involved the descriptor 'certainty.'

Chapter Twenty-Three

Maintaining Corporate Formalities

Are you willing to make the effort to minimize the bull's–eye on your business? Or are you a bit lazy? Is your attitude that if the bull's–eye grows, so be it? You're tough. You can stand a veil fail, and being held personally liable. If that's your attitude, be sure to check with your spouse and partners to see if they share it.

Laya v. Erin Homes, Inc. is an important case out of West Virginia.[49] Writing for the court, Justice McHugh made some very key points regarding corporate formalities, stating:

> In the context of a close corporation, the failure to follow corporate formalities is important because the trier of the facts may reasonably infer that such conduct springs not from merely innocent, overworked inattention to paperwork by the sole or controlling shareholder, but is indicative of the fact that such shareholder views the business as his or her own individual business so that there is no need to "go through the motions" of complying with formalities.
>
> Individuals who wish to enjoy limited personal liability for business activities under a corporate umbrella should be expected to adhere to the relatively simple formalities of creating and maintaining a corporate entity. In a sense, faithfulness to these formalities is the price paid for the corporate fiction, a relatively small price to pay for limited liability. Furthermore, the formalities are themselves

Chapter Twenty-Three

an excellent litmus of the extent to which the individuals involved actually view the corporation as a separate being...

Justice McHugh, I could not have said it better myself.

The Laya court then went on to enumerate their list of piercing factors, which are found in Appendix D. Like the Oakland Meat List, not all factors need to be present for a piercing.

But what should be present to avoid a piercing is what the court accurately described as an attitude. A mindset.

If you believe you don't need to follow the corporate formalities because you and the company are one, the court may more easily find against you. You've got the wrong attitude. On the other hand, recognizing entity separateness and following the formalities to prove up that separateness puts you ahead in the game. A corporate book filled with meeting minutes and properly issued share certificates clearly illustrates that you respect the difference between entity and self, and allows the court to respect it too. You've got the right mindset.

In this chapter we'll discuss the corporate formalities and how to prove them up.

In my years of experience helping people establish appropriate business structures, protect their assets, and limit their liability, I've seen that when a corporation is correctly operated and maintained, it can be key to helping individuals build and maintain wealth.

But that's the key word: Correctly. Unfortunately, you can't reap the many benefits of the corporate veil without maintaining all the formalities of a corporation, which formalities also apply to LLCs and LPs. Corporate formalities are the operating rules and guidelines that you must follow to meet the operational requirements of a corporation. If you fail to uphold them, as we've discussed, the veil can be pierced and personal liability imposed.

Still, many people make the mistake of being too loose and casual with the details of operating a corporation, LLC or LP (from here on we'll discuss corporations but, as before, know that the rules also apply to the other entities). Many owners lack written records of important decisions, forget to issue certificates of ownership, fail to hold organizational meetings, or, worse, commingle their business and personal funds, all of which leaves the veil vulnerable and too easily pierced. A lack of records also makes it harder when you are trying to sell your business. Attorneys for business buyers look down on scofflaw companies. Their attitude, prudently, is: "No documents. No deal."

In this chapter, we will discuss the basic actions you should take to get and keep your corporate house in order and ensure the veil remains intact.

Establish and Uphold Corporate Formalities

Appearances matter. In order for your corporation to be considered legitimate and benefit from the corporate veil, you have to act and look legitimate. For a small business, it can be tempting to dispense with the formalities, failing to designating officers (or managers) and a board of directors, have regular meetings, or keep written records, preferring instead to operate more casually and without labels. But without the formalities, it's hard to prove that you're operating the way a corporation should and thus would be entitled to its benefits.

It's essential that once you file your articles of incorporation seeking limited liability protection, that you follow certain practices to establish and maintain this status. If you don't, you are susceptible to a piercing of the veil because it will appear you are a corporation in name only—trying to take advantage of corporate benefits without earning the right to them.

What's considered a corporate formality? Here's a list:

1. Establishing a board of directors
2. Electing officers
3. Holding organizational meetings
4. Adopting company bylaws and procedures
5. Keeping accurate and detailed minutes and records
6. Announcing your corporate status to the world
7. Ensuring sufficient capital
8. Performing annual filings

Chapter Twenty-Three

9. Maintaining a distinction between corporate and personal assets

Let's look at each of these in detail.

Establish a Board of Directors

A company can't run without a leadership team to make decisions about how the business will operate. The board of directors plots the corporation's course, sets policies, performs an advisory role, and serves as the voice of the company. In an LLC the managers are both the board and the officers, and crucial to proper governance as discussed ahead. In an LP, the general partner runs the show.

All directors should be formally elected via an organizational meeting (which we'll discuss in a moment). Some states require a minimum number of directors, which is stated in the articles of incorporation, although in some states (such as Nevada and Wyoming) this minimum is one. Depending on the size of the board, you may opt to set up committees to address particular needs, such as audits or nominations of officers.

The size of the board depends on the size of the organization, the scope of the work to be done, or the value certain individuals bring to the table—there's no one size that every board of directors should be. However, it might be a good idea to include a required number of participants or a range it should fall between. For example, you might specify no fewer than three and no more than fifteen directors. You'll want to have an odd number of directors to avoid any deadlocks from tie votes. For example, a four-person board could vote 2 to 2 on a matter and then you are stuck.

The board's importance cannot be overstated: It sets up corporate policies, manages the business' affairs, and selects, supervises, and terminates its officers. It also oversees contracts, sales, and transfers of stocks and controls its money. Because of its important role, all board members must consent to serve; a person can't simply be installed in a board position without agreeing to accept it.

Verbal consent is generally acceptable, although you may opt to require written consent. In corporations subject to oversight by the Securities and Exchange Commission (SEC), generally publicly traded companies, written consent to serve on a board is required. Note also that consent to serve doesn't mean that director can't resign or be removed, but such actions should take place in writing.

Elect Officers

While the board presides over a company's operations from a high-level perspective, its officers manage the day-to-day business. This means that unlike individual directors, officers may act as agents on behalf of the corporation and elect for the company to enter into legally binding contractual relationships without risking personal liability. They function as executives of the corporation.

Typically, the officers include, at the very least, a president, secretary, and treasurer, although a vice president, chief executive officer (CEO), chief financial officer (CFO), controller, general manager, and assistant officers may be included, depending on the size of the organization and its needs. In some states, such as Nevada or Wyoming, one person may hold all of the offices. Your state and corporate bylaws should dictate the number of officers, which positions are required, and what each officer's basic duties are.

For your LLC: Manager Managed or Member Managed?

Should you be a member managed or manager managed LLC? Unlike a corporation, which must have a board of directors overseeing the officers managing the day to day operations, with the LLC you only have one layer of management, known as the manager(s). LLC flexibility allows for two types of managers—the member managed version where one or more members (owners) run the show and the manager managed method

Chapter Twenty-Three

whereby members or anyone else can manage the LLC. Of these two choices we suggest manager managed LLCs for three reasons.

First and foremost, manager managed LLCs are a way to prevent piercing the LLC veil and imposing personal liability on members for LLC obligations. As you know, corporations and LLCs can have their protections removed when the 'formalities' (the rules for proper operation) aren't followed.

A crucial element for piercing is showing that the LLC operators didn't respect the difference between ownership of the LLC and management of it. When member managers do everything themselves, as owners and management, the lines are blurred and the veil can fail.

By separating the management function, as a manager managed LLC does, from ownership the LLC is better able to provide a clear operational distinction. Having this argument in a piercing case is extremely valuable.

A second reason for manager managed is that the alternative can get confusing and messy. If you are member managed, does that mean all members have an equal say in management? Can every member bind the LLC to contracts?

In some scenarios, only certain members are designated as the member managers and the non managing members then get resentful of their second class status. The lines of authority are much clearer with manager management. Of course, the manager(s) can also be members and frequently are but operations are a step away from all the members and within the separate authority of the manager. Clarity and certainty are beneficial within any organization.

The third reason for manager managed involves convenience. When you file your initial paperwork with the state you must declare whether you will be member or manager managed. If you change from one method to another you must amend your formation articles. If you don't amend, problems could arise. Rather than face those issues, why not declare manager managed at the start? The members can always be managers. If the members later hire an outside professional manager you don't have to amend anything. The state already has you listed as a manager managed LLC. You have management flexibility right from the start.

To avoid the pierce, annually preparing minuets of meetings showing one or more persons both being elected to serve as managers and then managing the LLC for the benefit of the members is a useful defensive strategy.

Hold Organizational Meetings

Organizational meetings provide a great foundation for your corporate veil. You are showing your respect for required formalities and using the opportunity to make important decisions about how the business will be run, who will be responsible for what, what rules you will all abide by, how you will all be paid, and more.

Your first meeting is an important one. It should be done soon after your articles of incorporation are filed. After all, the first organizational meeting lays the groundwork for important legal aspects and functions of your corporation, including the members of your board, your officers, company bylaws (more on these in a bit), and issues involving your bank account, stock, and other financial information will be set forth.

All 50 states mandate that corporations also must hold at least an annual shareholder's meeting — even if there is only one shareholder — as well as an annual board of directors' meeting. Your corporate bylaws should specify when these meetings take place. Typically, the shareholders' meeting is first, because this is where the board for the coming year is elected. The board meeting often comes afterward, usually on the same day, perhaps even immediately following, so that the directors and officers can formally accept their positions for the year and address company business.

As developments occur in the business, special meetings may also be required in order to make decisions — urgent matters such as opening bank accounts, approving a lease obligation, adopting a new tax year, hiring a new vendor, or ratifying a real estate acquisition. Special meetings must be executed according to the rules stated in your company bylaws, with due notice of the meeting, usually between 10 and 60 days beforehand,

Chapter Twenty-Three

being given to participants as required. Know that notice can be waived in writing by the directors (or manager in an LLC) if the meeting needs to occur quickly.

The standard steps for properly holding a meeting of directors or shareholders are:

1. Call for meeting: The meeting is called or requested by someone who is authorized to do so or in accordance with the bylaws. Your state may have requirements about which individuals are empowered to call shareholders' or directors' meetings, and your bylaws should address how often meetings should be held.

2. Provide notice: Notice of the meeting date, time, and location is provided to directors and shareholders. Written notice is preferred and emails may be acceptable. The larger the corporation, the more a formal written announcement will be important. Your bylaws may or may not state how much notice must be given but, again, typically the range is between 10 and 60 days. Providing ample notice should be considered as a matter of courtesy. It should be given enough ahead of time that the shareholders and directors can plan to attend, and for participants to review any background materials that may be discussed. Note that if you hold a meeting telephonically or virtually (via Zoom, for example), the details about how to join should be spelled out in detail.

3. Share necessary materials: An agenda and/or other meeting materials are distributed along with the meeting notice, so that participants have the opportunity to review them or request clarification. These materials may include copies of presentation or background materials, treasurer's reports to be discussed, proposed corporate resolutions, minutes from prior meetings that need approval, or, in certain cases that may have particular importance or be controversial. An Acknowledgement of Receipt of Notice of Meeting form may be provided. Such a notice would be signed and returned as a protective measure, demonstrating that all those invited to the meeting were provided notice, should there

Maintaining Corporate Formalities

be a question about it later. And again, a waiver of notice for an immediately needed meeting should be signed by all participants.

4. Hold meeting: The meeting is held according to the agenda or predetermined subject matter. The secretary should keep notes of the meeting, particularly regarding important decisions made or votes taken. Your organization should establish a minimum number of directors or shareholders that must be present at a meeting in order to take action, otherwise known as a quorum, and include this in your bylaws. Typically, this comes to just over one half of the total number of positions—for example, on a board of 15 directors, a quorum would be at least eight—although for small organizations, you might opt for two-thirds (for example, three members of a five-person board). If a quorum is not present, or if someone leaves and breaks quorum, the meeting should be adjourned and action taken at a later time.

5. Provide minutes: Minutes of the meeting are prepared, signed, and stored with corporate records. Often, as a courtesy to those attending, the minutes are read aloud or reviewed at the next meeting and approved. Occasionally, there may be small corrections to be made, but this is an efficient means by which to bring attendees up to speed and summarize discussions and decisions made previously. As well, this written record, kept in safe place, can be used to show your faithfulness in complying with corporate formalities.

Adopt Bylaws and Procedures

Your bylaws are your internal (meaning: not filed with the state or other agency) document that states the rules to which your corporation will adhere. Bylaw language should address:

1. Requirements regarding notice for, number of, and dates of organizational meetings

2. Rules regarding the election, appointment, and removal of officers and directors

Chapter Twenty-Three

3. Rights, duties, and privileges of the directors, officers, members, or shareholders
4. Number of members needed to maintain a quorum
5. Whether you will designate committees and for what
6. How stocks will be issued or transferred
7. Provisions indemnifying directors and officers from liability
8. Rules regarding how conflicts of interest will be disclosed or handled
9. Processes for making amendments to bylaws
10. Procedures for shareholders' inspection of corporate records
11. Name and address of the corporation's resident agent (without one, your corporate veil may be pierced)

The bottom line is that failure to observe and uphold corporate bylaws could diminish the protections offered under the corporate veil. A good attorney trying to pierce will argue: Why grant limited liability to a company so limited that they can't even follow their own rules?

Essentially, the bylaws are your company's operating manual, and their existence ensures the security of your corporate veil by demonstrating the legitimacy and accountability of your organization. Though they may not be required by your state's laws, courts often check for bylaws if there are disputes within the company. However, bylaws should not be too complicated nor provide for overly intricate procedures. You want to operate under them, not be suppressed by them.

In the context of an LLC, the operating agreement serves as the bylaws, a road map for how the entity will operate. Generally, an operating agreement is more flexible and can provide for more unique agreements than can corporate bylaws. Work with a good attorney to draft your operating agreement for maximized benefits, and then follow the rules you have set forth.

It's common for corporations to update their bylaws as their business grows and evolves. If you wish to add, delete, or change certain provisions, this is fairly easy to do. In most states, certain amendments only need to be approved by directors, although the shareholders may also have the power to do so as long as it is consistent with state law. Amendments can usually pass with a simple majority vote, and the vote should be documented in meeting minutes. If the amendment passes, a resolution should be written explaining the changes in complete detail, and the change goes into effect immediately. Be sure to update the official bylaws as soon as possible to prevent confusion.

Maintain Careful Minutes and Records

Of course, without keeping written records of your corporation's activities and discussions, it's very hard to demonstrate that you're operating in accordance with your articles of incorporation and bylaws. Properly keeping accurate, detailed minutes of meetings and written records of transactions or decisions is one the most important ways to ensure your veil cannot be pierced. It also ensures that members of the organization adhere to decisions made and communicates important news to shareholders.

In certain corporate matters, discretion and confidentiality are important. But as history has shown us, too many corporations have gone down in flames for destroying or hiding records or even telling employees not to record certain information. A paper trail is always a safe bet. If you look like you might be hiding something, you'll raise suspicion, even if it's merely an oversight. Get into the habit of keeping careful records. They will be your friends.

Minutes are a formal record of a meeting summarizing the essential actions taken by the board or incorporators. For example, the minutes from your first organizational meeting may show what decisions are made regarding taxes (the corporation's accounting period and tax year, for instance), the details of your first stock issuance, approval of the corporate seal or stock certificates, and approval of other business-formation decisions such as bylaws, bank account openings, and the like.

Any official directors' or shareholders' meeting—whether regularly scheduled or special— should be documented with minutes. These should be described in enough detail that it's clear what decisions have been made or actions taken, and minutes should be read aloud to ensure objections or

Chapter Twenty-Three

clarifications are addressed, as a courtesy as well as to maintain accurate records.

However, many corporations hold impromptu meetings all the time and don't record minutes. That's absolutely fine. But any time matters of a legal or financial nature are discussed, particularly in which decisions consequential are made, those discussions should be recorded. As well, you should have written minutes of your annual meetings to prove you are following the law.

Minutes should be kept in a log book or other standardized location (which include electronic storage) that serve as the corporate memory storehouse, which is important because some of these may be subpoenaed by the courts or reviewed for auditing purposes. In light of this, it's a good idea to write minutes as if they will be read by the person you'd least like to have read them.

Resolutions are another type of record that should be maintained by corporations. A resolution is a document that records actions that the directors or shareholders resolve to take on the corporation's behalf. Resolutions should be issued to authorize business transactions (such as opening a bank account or approving a contract), address tax reporting changes (such as electing S-Corp status or changing the corporation's tax year), amend bylaws or articles of incorporation, hire employees or contractors, address conflicts of interest, seek loan funding or make loans, make changes to benefits or reimbursements, issue dividends, issue stocks, or seek professional counsel (such as from an attorney).

If a decision must be made or action taken but those involved determine, for whatever reason, that an actual meeting cannot be held, an alternative would be to authorize action by written consent. This is a quick but effective way to document formal corporate action. The directors and/or shareholders would sign a document that provides the language of the corporation's decision or resolution. By signing it, those directors or shareholders approve the language. To ensure the action by written consent is appropriately documented, the relevant parties would sign the consent form (consenting to an immediate meeting without following the regular notice provisions) which should be kept with the corporate minutes.

176

Maintaining Corporate Formalities

Announce Your Corporate Status to the World

As discussed throughout, appearances matter. Large efforts, such as establishing boards and issuing stocks demonstrate your corporate status, but so do smaller efforts like printing business cards and company letterhead and sharing news of corporate activity from the perspective of the company rather than the individuals. Individual directors and officers may be subject to personal liability if they act on the corporation's behalf without being up front about doing so. And communications about corporate activities should clearly be seen as coming from the company. Invoices, company checks, brochures, and the like, should identify the corporation, as should contracts and correspondences, which should be signed with both names and titles to distinguish corporate actions. Don't sign a business contract as simply 'John Jones.' Instead, the signature line should read:

> John Jones, President
> John Jones, Inc.

These simple steps aren't about vanity. Instead, they send a message to the world that your corporation is distinct from those individuals who comprise it. By signing as just 'John Jones' you are giving an attorney the argument that their client thought they were dealing with you as an individual ('John Jones') instead of as a company ('John Jones, Inc.') If they can argue they thought you were acting as an individual all of your personal assets are exposed.

Ensure Sufficient Capital

Just as you, as an individual, need to demonstrate that you have sufficient income to cover expenses when you purchase a vehicle or home, apply for a loan, or ask for a line of credit, your corporation must demonstrate that it can pay its bills, too. This means ensuring that it is sufficiently capitalized to begin and as you continue operating. Paying dividends to shareholders may be a test of sufficient capitalization as well—the Model

Chapter Twenty-Three

Business Corporation Act forbids the paying of dividends if it results in the inability to pay debts as they become due, or if its liabilities outweigh its assets.

What's considered "sufficient capital"? This is a moving target that depends on many factors, some of which we discussed in Chapter 16 on undercapitalization. Sufficient capital should be able to cover short-term expenses—purchasing supplies and equipment, paying salaries, keeping its lights on, and the like. This indicates that the company can indeed operate independently of its individual owners and its initial money sources. But what if those sources obligate the company to more than they've brought in to 'just see' if the company can make it? What if those sources drain the accounts to the detriment of vendors and customers? Guess what? The court is likely to pierce the corporate veil. In fact, courts in some states, including California, have relied on undercapitalization as a primary reason for piercing.

Plus, it's just good business: The inability to effectively manage working capital is one of the top reasons businesses fail.

Of course, it's reasonable to expect money to be tight as a start up business is just getting off the ground. But a certain amount of investment at the outset is important to demonstrate that you are building a legitimate corporation and can cover its initial costs and liabilities. You'll need to manage your working capital by carefully monitoring your inventory and keeping a close eye on accounts payable and accounts receivable.

To properly manage all of this, it's a good idea to employ a bookkeeper or accountant. Exercise discipline to ensure that money is spent on only what is essential to the business, particularly if capital is tight. Never spend business monies for personal expenses. Developing and adhering to a strict budget is essential, including building in a cushion for unforeseen expenditures. Also important is paying employees on time (as is legally required) as well as vendors, which builds goodwill. Regarding vendors, timely payment helps to plant the seeds for future benefits whereby bulk discounts or other benefits are offered to the corporation because of the healthy financial relationship.

Maintaining Corporate Formalities

Keep a tight rein on credit extended to customers. If you're going to offer it, it should be controlled and enforced vigorously, or you could be unwillingly subjecting yourself to insufficient capitalization risks due to someone else's nonpayment. Remember, if you're not paid within 60 days there's a good chance you will never collect. Don't let the deadbeats bring you down.

Perform Annual Filings

Some business owners, after filing their articles of incorporation, rest too comfortably in the notion that their filings are complete, and in so doing fail to adhere to the deadlines of the ongoing annual filings. You've got to pay to play and most states charge a reasonable fee for your continued entity protection. In Wyoming it is $62 a year. In California the franchise fee is $800 a year. Failure to complete these filings (and pay the fees) in a timely manner can lead to a variety of penalties, not the least of which is suspension of your corporate charter. This would prohibit you from entering into contracts, filing or defending yourself in lawsuits, or, in some states, doing any business at all. The time, energy and expense devoted to establishing the corporation will all have been wasted if the state revokes your corporate charter for failing to perform the timely (and very simple) annual filings. While it may be possible to have your charter reinstated, the best way to ensure your corporate veil remains intact and the corporation serves its purpose is to perform these filings on time. Again, this is not hard to do.

Almost all states require specific annual filings with their secretaries of state. A business must be aware of what filings to make initially as well as periodically. Some states, for example, require businesses to file annual documentation to ensure they retain their corporate status. Some states ask corporations to keep certain documents in their own files for a fixed number of years. Professional corporations, which are comprised of professionals in specialized areas, such as doctors, attorneys, or engineers, may have separate annual filings to identify professional employees and

Chapter Twenty-Three

address malpractice insurance coverage. Because every state and type of corporation has its own unique requirements, it's your job to find out what's required when and stay on top of them.

In general, states want to be kept apprised of current directors, officers, address, and resident (or registered) agents of corporations. Deadlines vary, with some requiring this to be done annually and others biannually or other periodic schedules. This is usually done in an annual report filed with the secretary of state. Publicly traded companies often publish extensive annual reports that detail valuable information for shareholders pertaining to the corporation's financial status, recent changes made within the company, and projections as to future performance. But rest assured that the required annual report filing for most business owners and investors is usually a lot simpler than that. Rather, it's usually just a straightforward document that calls for any updates in names or contact information for directors, officers, and registered agents. You may also need to include information about the number of outstanding shares or other related matters. Please also know that the US Treasury Department will be requiring an annual report from every entity (with only a few exceptions) beginning in 2022.

Note that while some states may require printed and signed hard copies of these forms, others may allow them to be submitted electronically. Filing as dictated by your state, in the time and manner required, is an essential corporate formality. You don't want to give any outsider the argument that there was a time when your corporation wasn't current and your veil was weak.

Maintain a Distinction Between Corporate and Personal Assets

Perhaps the most visible—and most dangerous—breach of the corporate veil is the failure to maintain a distinction between corporate and personal assets. The consequences of commingling these assets can be fatal for the corporation.

Maintaining Corporate Formalities

In 2002, which is often referred to in business circles as "The Year of the Scandal," Tyco International became an infamous example of the dangers of commingling assets, which took place on multiple occasions. CEO Dennis Kozlowski utilized Tyco funds for personal expenses, such as houses, artwork, and even his wife's extravagant birthday party. Kozlowski exploited loopholes that had been built into its corporate structure—holes that have been closed pursuant to the Sarbanes-Oxley Act— including a general lack of oversight as well as the existence of programs that allowed for executive loans or other funding.

Suffice it to say that auditors and courts are highly sensitive to commingling now and are on high alert to its signs. Too many small business owners unfortunately find themselves somewhere in the middle between full corporate accounting and a broad range of personal transactions, failing to draw a clear red line between them. As a corporation is getting off the ground, owners may be tempted to pull company assets for personal use, having every intention to pay it back and stay on the up and up. As you know by now, this is asking for trouble.

A corporation must maintain a separate financial identity. It must have its own bank account, file separate tax returns, and use corporate assets exclusively for corporate purposes. The company should not be used as a lender or pay master for its officers, directors, or shareholders, those known as insiders. Skirting these rules is not only a bad ethical practice but, along with other factors, it may lead to a piercing. No one affiliated with the business should ever consider corporation property as personally accessible, as they have that fiduciary duty, that duty of trust, to the company.

What constitutes commingling? Here are a few typical scenarios:
1. Having one account for both personal and business use
2. Writing business checks for personal expenses, or personal checks for business expenses
3. Depositing business checks into your personal account
4. Transferring money between business and personal accounts without documentation

Chapter Twenty-Three

Commingling makes it hard for the courts to determine where the company stops and your personal life begins, leading them to see the business as merely an alter ego rather than a separate entity.

It can open up an individual to civil liabilities, and even criminal charges such as fraud or embezzlement.

There are a few simple steps you can take to ensure commingling doesn't take place:

1. Establish a bank account specifically for the company.
2. Carefully document all expenses, withdrawals, and deposits associated with the account. Work with your bookkeeper on this. This provides accountability and helps you to track your business' performance and where spending is occurring.
3. Deposit receivables into business accounts and pay yourself (complete with payroll withholding) through the business.
4. Pay for business supplies and equipment with the business account only.

There's an additional benefit to keeping a brick wall between business and personal accounts: It makes filing tax returns much simpler. When the IRS, as guided by your accountant, can clearly see business income and expenses separate from those returns that are personal, you are in the compliance zone. Which is a good place to be.

As you know by now: Corporate formalities are important. They are easy. Follow them.

Chapter Twenty-Four

How to Stay Protected

As we have learned, when parent corporations and their subsidiary children get too close courts may pierce the veil. Brother, sister and other closely related companies doing the same can also suffer a piercing. And sister companies, even if one is dead, can be merged together to create a new life as a Sister Frankenstein candidate for piercing.

Clearly it is important to know how to stay on the safe side of things. While when it comes to piercing we can never be exactly sure what any court will do, it stands to reason that there must be some facts that the courts like to see to rule **against** a piercing. Along with the corporate formalities discussed in the last chapter, these factors, discussed here, are financial autonomy, intercompany agreements, record retention, management separation and signs of sovereignty.

1. Financial Autonomy

As the cases indicate, the undercapitalized subsidiary of a prosperous parent can be pierced to reach the parent's assets. Alter ego liability frequently provides the rationale.

What if each subsidiary was adequately capitalized, especially upon formation, to fund its startup and on-going losses? What if each subsidiary had assets exceeding liabilities and could pay its debts as they became due? A subsidiary's veil will never be pierced if it can pay its own way.

183

Chapter Twenty-Four

Financial autonomy includes maintaining separate bank accounts and paying the subsidiary's bills from the subsidiary's own bank account. Leases and other obligations should be in the subsidiary's corporate name. Only officers of the subsidiary (and not the parent) should have signatory authority for the subsidiary's financial accounts.

A piercing factor some courts look to is the commingling of monies between parent and sub. Separate accounts can help negate the argument, as can a policy of preparing separate profit and loss statements and balance sheets for each entity.

Be careful on distributions. A dominate shareholder taking monies from a sub that should have flowed through to the parent can evidence a lack of financial autonomy.

While you may not think such formalities are important or necessary 'you' are not who we are doing all these for. You are doing it for a future attorney and judge looking into how you are conducting your company's affairs. You want to show separate autonomies.

2. Intercompany Agreements

When a parent uses its subsidiary's assets or services without some sort of payment courts are more likely to pierce. If the parent doesn't respect the subsidiary's sovereignty, then why shouldn't a creditor, left unpaid by the sub, be able to go after the parent? If the parent company had properly paid the sub there may have been enough money for the creditor to collect from the subsidiary.

Intercompany agreements (or 'ICAs') are contracts by and between two or more subsidiaries or divisions owned by the same parent company. The term 'intercompany' refers to the internal nature of any sales of goods and services between the related companies. You won't enter into an ICA with an independent third party. For that, you'll use a regular contract. Within a company, ICAs can cover a wide range of transactions from back-office services to intellectual property licensing to cost and revenue sharing agreements.

How to Stay Protected

ICAs may involve your CPA or tax advisor. Typically, companies don't profit from intercompany sales as, for the most part, goods and services are being internally transferred within the same tax paying entity without any tax consequence. Still, the IRS likes to see arm's length terms that are similar to those of unrelated parties.

Things get more complicated when you do business overseas and the issue of transfer pricing comes into play. Transfer pricing asks the question: Where is the profit made? In the USA parent or in the offshore subsidiary? If the ICA calls for most of the profit to be made in a low tax jurisdiction and very little profit to be made in a high tax jurisdiction, who investigates? Not the low tax country. They don't really care about the taxes. They're just glad you're employing people and assets in their country. But the high tax country sure does care, and they'll send investigators out to look at your ICAs and determine whether they reflect market standards or not. Is the U.S. side making its fair share of the profit? The IRS asks this question. They want to tax a dollar of profit, not a dime. You will work with your tax advisor to make sure the transfer pricing policies in your ICAs are fair and reasonable. Also know that not having the right ICAs in place during a government investigation can put you in a bad spot.

As a general rule, the following are the basics found in each ICA:

1. Parties
2. Consideration (an exchange of value)
3. Arm's length payment
4. Term
5. Taxation
6. Governing laws and jurisdictions

A key ICA for many businesses involves intellectual property (or 'IP'). Your patents, trademarks, copyrights, trade secrets and domain names need extra protection. We don't want a litigant to sue your operating company and reach the IP that allows you to succeed in business. Instead, have the IP held, in most cases, in a Wyoming LLC and use ICAs to license out the rights to the various related companies.

A chart illustrates the scenario:

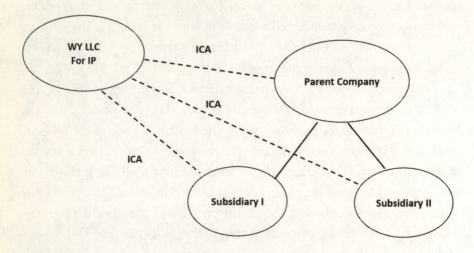

If the parent company or one of the subs gets sued the valuable IP is in a stand-alone LLC. The litigant never did business with the Wyoming LLC and has no right to sue it directly. With ICAs in place providing market rates for the license of IP rights we have a legitimate, arms-length transaction. A litigant trying to pierce a parent or a sub to reach the valuable IP rights inside the Wyoming LLC will have a difficult time. The entity and the ICA agreement provide a clear separation between the other subs and the parent.

Know that many entrepreneurs hold their intellectual property in this more protected format.

They know the value of their IP.

3. Record Retention

It is difficult to assert your veil when your records are gone. Record retention is not only an important defensive strategy it is in many cases a legal requirement.

How to Stay Protected

Accounting records are subject to some of the strictest rules. In terms of basic guidelines, consider the following:

7 Year Hold	Permanent Hold
Bank statements / Deposit slips	Auditor's reports
Taxes (Payroll)	Annual financial statements
Payroll records	Taxes (Income)
Electronic payment records	Cash disbursements
Employee expense reports	Cash receipt journal
Freight / Bill of lading	Chart of accounts
Inventory listings and tags	Deeds, mortgages, bills of sale
Time cards	Fixed asset records
	General journal
	General ledger
	Training manuals

Thankfully these records can be now kept electronically. But with all the hacking and ransomware and lack of computer security in the world, permanently seems like a long, uncertain time. Do your best.

You are also going to want to keep your entity documents—articles, bylaws or operating agreements and ownership certificates—on a multiyear hold. The exact time frame may be governed by considerations involving the statute of limitations (the time period in which to bring a claim). One of the longest statutes of limitations you will face, for example, is the ten year period in which to bring a claim for construction defects. If you are building, remodeling or even flipping houses you will want to keep your entity documents that long.

Similarly, for property records, the generally accepted retention schedule is to keep your records relating to property until the period of limitation expires for the year in which you dispose of the property in a taxable disposition. The underlying rationale is that you must keep these records to figure your adjusted basis for computing gain or loss when you sell or otherwise dispose of the property. You will also want your entity

187

Chapter Twenty-Four

documents to prove that the tax paying title holding entity properly existed.

Know that each state has a different requirement for how long your entity documents must be kept. Wyoming mandates a permanent hold, Nevada is vague on the topic and Delaware does not statutorily require any such keeping. Prudence would dictate a long term hold.

4. Management Separation

A goal for parent corporations should be to minimize the amount of control they have over a subsidiary's day to day operations. Parental control does not mean an entirely hands off attitude. General corporate policies including, for example, a consistent employee handbook for all subsidiaries, are acceptable, as is a parent exercising some measures of supervision over their subsidiaries.

The key is to avoid a domination, whereby a parent exercises such an intrusive hands-on control that the subsidiary is left with little responsibility for its own affairs. When the parent makes all subsidiary business decisions without involving the subsidiary's management team problems may arise.

Be aware of any overlap in directors and officers within a parent/ subsidiary or a brother/sister scenario. If the subsidiary has one director in common with the parent for oversight and policy consistency goals that will be fine. But if all of the officers and directors are the same people for two separate entities, courts will question the level of control exercised by the parent. It can be difficult to assert a subsidiary's independence when the same gang is closely running both shows. Senior executives providing management services solely to the subsidiary should be directly employed by the subsidiary. As well, each subsidiary should make its own determinations for the employment and termination of officers and employees.

Establishing clean lines of separation between parent and sub, sister and brother, will entail a bit more extra work but will provide plenty more protection.

5. Signs of Sovereignty

Courts will consider evidence as to whether third parties see a parent and sub as separate entities or as a complete single entity. As such, showing separate sovereignties, in all facets of operations, becomes important.

Can your subsidiary afford its own logo and website? Using letterhead and office signage with a logo distinct from the parent gains separation. So does having a unique website offering management email addresses different than the parent. Any invoices should request payment to be made directly to the subsidiary's office or direct deposit account.

We have spoken about common office space in previous chapters. If only one office is used, a sublease agreement providing for actual payments from subsidiary to parent should be in writing and signed by the appropriate respective officers. The lease payments should actually be paid each month. If possible, the sub should have its own phone number to further highlight entity differences.

As we discussed in Chapter 22, in France they will pierce the veil under the doctrine of the appearance of corporate groups. The same doctrine applies here. If all of your entities appear as one with the same offices, office phone numbers, and the like—legally, in the eyes of the court, they actually become one, as a single enterprise responsible for everything. Good attorneys and judges will notice this fusion. Don't allow them to call forth Sister Frankenstein to haunt your dreams and take your assets.

Instead, present the signs of sovereignty with each entity. Make it abundantly clear, so that a future judge or jury can easily see, that your corporations, LLCs and LPs are distinct and separate from each other. By following these important strategies—attention to corporate formalities, financial autonomy, intercompany agreements, record retention, management separation and clear signs of sovereignty—you will help to significantly protect yourself from a piercing claim. Veil not fail.

Conclusion

Your business has a bull's—eye on it. As we've learned, that bull's—eye never goes away. It remains on every business and asset holding entity as a target for anyone suing to hit and perforate into your personal asset column.

We want to minimize that target. We want to make it very hard for anyone to challenge your hard-earned assets. Let the 50% success rate for piercing the veil fall against those who don't follow the rules.

You've read the horror stories, and now you know what not to do. You have learned the defensive strategies, the relatively simple steps involving corporate formalities and separateness, that shrinks the bull's—eye and keeps your personal assets sheltered from business attacks. You now know how to follow these rules. And you will follow them.

Your veil will not fail. You will stay protected,

Good luck in all your endeavors.

Appendix A

The Law of Fraudulent Transfers
By Ted Sutton

Introduction

What happens when a creditor tries to collect on a judgment, and learns that the debtor does not have any assets? The laws against fraudulent transfers may be used to assist the creditor.

Debt collection is an age-old issue. In order to protect creditors from debtors who made suspicious transfers, the English Parliament adopted the first fraudulent transfer statute in 1571.[1] Since then, fraudulent transfer law has evolved to better deal with the questionable transfers of today. In 1918, many states adopted the Uniform Fraudulent Conveyance Act (UFCA). Later in the 20th century, another change was made to reflect the debtor-creditor trends of the time. In 1984, the UFCA was overhauled by the Uniform Fraudulent Transfer Act (UFTA), which 43 states have adopted. The other seven states have their own similar rules. In 2014, the Uniform Voidable Transactions Act (UVTA) overhauled the UFTA

One type of transmission that the UVTA encompasses is an actual fraudulent transfer, which occurs when the debtor makes a transfer either with an actual intent to hinder, delay, or defraud the creditor, or if the debtor did not receive a reasonably equivalent value in exchange for the transfer.[2]

It is difficult for creditors to use direct evidence to prove a fraudulent transfer.[3] Getting defendants to freely admit their malicious intent is not easy. To counter this dilemma, the UVTA provides a nonexclusive list of eleven "badges of fraud." Much to the relief of creditors and their lawyers, these badges allow a creditor circumstantially to prove whether a debtor's

Appendix A

transfer was actually fraudulent, whereby the factors prove the wrong. Each fraud marker is discussed ahead, with one case being used to describe common fact patterns for each badge. We have not changed the names of the parties, as before. Most of the cases are analyzed under the UFTA, the uniform law that pre-dates the more recent UVTA. It is also worth noting that a few cases discussed here pre-date the UFTA. However, each case is still relevant because they incorporate scenarios of what the different badges of fraud are designed to protect creditors against.

These eleven cases will provide a sense of how courts have treated certain fraudulent transfers under both older fraudulent transfer law and the UVTA's badges of fraud regime.

The UVTA Badges of Fraud

1. The transfer or obligation was to an insider

The first badge of fraud involves cases where the debtor makes a transfer or obligation to an insider. The term "insider" is used in a very broad sense, and can include anyone who has some sort of control over a debtor. To show just how broadly the term is used, courts have determined that an unmarried cohabiting partner can be an insider. A case out of Ohio, *Slone v. Lassiter (In re Grove- Merritt)*, helps establish this proposition.[4]

In *Slone*, Devon Grove-Merritt, the debtor, and her husband purchased a home financed by a mortgage. The following year, Devon and her husband separated and ultimately divorced. Christo Lassiter, the defendant, was the debtor's former law professor. Christo assisted Devon in the divorce proceedings and eventually began a romantic relationship with her. After the divorce, the former husband transferred his one-half undivided interest in the home through a quitclaim deed to Devon, who in turn transferred that same interest to Christo. Over time, Devon accrued over $30,000 in credit card debt. In order to shield her assets from creditors, she transferred her remaining one-half undivided interest in the home to Christo through a quitclaim deed.

Devon then filed for Chapter 7 bankruptcy in the Ohio Southern Bankruptcy Court. In determining whether the debtor was liable for transferring this interest, the court examined whether the defendant was an insider under Ohio's UFTA. The court defined an insider as someone who has a sufficiently close relationship with the debtor where the insider is in a position to exercise some degree of control over the debtor, and is thus subject to closer scrutiny than someone dealing at arm's length with the debtor.

The court cited ample evidence to determine that Christo had a close relationship and exercised enough control over Devon. Christo had pressured Devon to transfer her interest in the home to him, had sought legal advice on what to do with Devon's situation, and had also been substantially involved in many of Devon's affairs. The court concluded that Christo, as an unmarried cohabiting partner, was in fact an insider under Ohio's fraudulent transfer laws. As a result, the transfer was avoided and the creditors collected the one-half undivided interest worth over $11,000. While some relationships like these might not seem to meet the requirements of an "insider", the UVTA finds ways to void many of these transactions under its broad definition.

2. The debtor retained possession or control of the property transferred after the transfer

The debtor's retaining possession or control of the property transferred after the transfer is the second badge of fraud. There are many different factual scenarios in which this type of fraud is present.

One interesting case involving this badge is *Tronox Inc. v. Kerr McGee Corp.*, which deals with a company that attempted to offload its environmental liabilities.[5]

Tronox was a very contentious case. It involved over 6,000 exhibits, thousands of pages of deposition testimony, and the trial lasted for 34 days. More importantly, the *Tronox* case had an interesting timeline. Kerr-McGee Corporation was founded in 1929 as an oil and gas exploration

Appendix A

company. By 2005, Kerr-McGee had two main businesses. One was a profitable oil and gas exploration and production (E&P) business. The other was an unprofitable chemical business that produced titanium dioxide, an industrial chemical used to whiten products. By this time, Kerr-McGee had significant environmental liabilities. They were responsible for remediating more than 2,700 environmental sites in 47 different states, and had spent more than $160 million on remediation costs.

In 2002, Anadarko, another company, strongly considered purchasing Kerr-McGee, but concluded that it would be unprofitable due to their environmental liabilities. Lehman Brothers, a New York investment bank that filed for bankruptcy in the 2008 economic crisis, advised that the profitable E&P business could be transferred into a new company in order to disclaim the environmental obligations. As a collateral move, Kerr-McGee formed a subsidiary company named Tronox Worldwide LLC (Tronox) in 2005. This company held both the titanium dioxide business and the environmental liabilities.

After these moves were made, Kerr-McGee continued to have control over Tronox, and repeatedly underfunded its liabilities. In fact, Tronox could never pay for the liabilities that Kerr-McGee was once able to afford. Moreover, the titanium dioxide business was never profitable.

Given their financial troubles, Tronox, as a debtor-in-possession, filed for Chapter 11 bankruptcy in 2009. Their complaint set forth eleven claims for relief, one of which was that Kerr-McGee made constructive fraudulent transfers under the Oklahoma UFTA. At the trial level, the court found that Tronox adequately stated a claim for relief under the Oklahoma UFTA. This question was revisited on appeal.

The Second Circuit Court of Appeals reviewed the facts of the case under the 11 badges of fraud, including whether the debtor retained possession or control of the property after the transfer. Here, as seen through the facts, the court found that Kerr-McGee retained complete possession and control of Tronox. Kerr-McGee had control over the liabilities transferred into Tronox and had influence over Tronox's management. Kerr-McGee also held 88.7% of Tronox's combined voting power. Based on these findings, the Second Circuit Court of Appeals affirmed the holding of the trial court, and Kerr- McGee was held liable under the Oklahoma UFTA. The Second Circuit Court of Appeals allowed Tronox to settle a judgment and collect a significant amount of damages from Kerr-McGee. Debtors having this level of control will be held liable under the UVTA.

3. The transfer or obligation was concealed

The next badge of fraud occurs when the debtor conceals the transfer. A debtor conceals a transfer when they omit assets from financial statements, especially when they are given to creditors or bankruptcy trustees. These types of transfers occur when debtors experience serious financial difficulties. Many of these situations present themselves in bankruptcy proceedings. Bankruptcy trustees can be tenacious in seeking out assets. *In Re Taylor* is one such case that comes out of Utah.[6]

Harold Taylor was a successful real estate investor in Park City, Utah. Over time, he began to experience health issues. He suffered both a heart attack and a stroke, and began receiving social security benefits. Due to his health conditions, his real estate business saw a rapid decline in income, prompting Harold to file for bankruptcy.

Two weeks before filing for bankruptcy, in seeking to shield his assets, Harold transferred his one-half interest in his Jeep to his wife. He needed to shield himself from creditors. His home did not have a mortgage on it, and it was subject to the creditors in the bankruptcy proceeding. Harold did not disclose the Jeep transfer to the court. The United States District Court for the District of Utah analyzed this transfer under the UFTA badges of fraud, and found that the Jeep transfer was a concealed fraudulent conveyance. The court set aside the transfer.

Harold's wife appealed the case to the Tenth Circuit Court of Appeals. After reviewing the facts, the court found that Harold concealed the transfer of the Jeep when he neither disclosed the transaction nor listed the transfer as an asset when he filed for bankruptcy. The court affirmed the judgment respecting Harold's Jeep transaction. Cases like these show

Appendix A

that it is not wise to hide such transactions from the court, even something as seemingly insignificant as a used car.

4. Before the transfer was made or obligation incurred, the debtor had been sued or threatened with suit

When a debtor has either been sued or is threatened with suit is when the next fraud marker arises. This is very common in divorce cases. One such case is *Breitenstine v. Breitenstine*, out of Wyoming.[7] In *Breitenstine*, an Ohio couple was married with two children. After the wife went on a hunting trip to Jackson Hole, she and the husband decided to purchase a home in Jackson worth $2.2 million. Shortly thereafter, their relationship began to deteriorate and the parties separated. Given these troubles, the husband secretly set up an offshore family trust in the Bahamas to transfer all of the marital assets. Most of the marital estate came by way of inheritance from the husband's parents, and it was worth at least $8.7 million. After several years of separating and reconciling, the wife filed for divorce in the District Court of Teton County, Wyoming. The District Court ordered a property division in favor of the wife, and the husband appealed to the Supreme Court of Wyoming.

Determining a proper dollar amount for alimony and child support involves knowing what is owned. The husband never disclosed that he held a valuable trust, instead claiming that his net worth was substantially smaller. Eventually, the trust was found, along with many badges of fraud. In particular, the court focused on the suspicious timing of the trust. After all, the husband formed the trust after he and his wife were separated, and then continually transferred assets into it up until the time they were divorced. Clearly, the husband was on notice of any threatened litigation by his wife. The court ultimately ordered the husband to assign the property to his wife to satisfy the alimony and child support payments. It is problematic to make such transfers before a lawsuit.

198

The Law of Fraudulent Transfers

5. *The transfer was of substantially all the debtor's assets*

The fifth designation of deceit involves the transfer of substantially all of the debtor's assets. Many of these cases arise when the debtor is experiencing financial trouble, such as bankruptcy or an indebtedness to a financial institution. One case that accurately describes this factual scenario is *Washington Trust Bank v. Erickson*, where the debtor was in severe financial trouble, and set up a trust to shield his financial assets from creditors.[8]

In *Erickson*, Marvin Erickson set up a trust for the benefit of his children when he began having health issues in 2008. Then, in 2010, the Ericksons found themselves significantly indebted to several banks, and certainly faced the prospect of litigation from the banks. In response to this threat, Marvin transferred substantially all of his assets into the trust to shield them from the banks. These assets included significant personal property, their primary residence, and other real property parcels. When these transfers were made, the Ericksons were indebted to two banks in an amount over $800,000. These transfers resulted in a significant change in the Erickson's net worth. In 2009, their net worth was listed over $10.8 million. In 2010, however, their net worth was negative by over $100,000.

Washington Trust Bank ("WTB") filed a complaint in 2011 in Idaho's Kootenai County District Court, and a motion for partial summary judgment was granted in 2012. In WTB's reply in support of their motion for partial summary judgment, they alleged that, under the UFTA and all of its badges of fraud, the Ericksons' transfers consisted of virtually all of their assets.

The court had an easy time reviewing this badge of fraud. After the transfers were made into the Erickson's trust between 2009 and 2010, the Erickson's net worth was reduced by over 89%. The court found that these transfers were of substantially all of the Erickson's assets. Along with finding other badges of fraud associated with these transfers, the court granted partial summary judgment in favor of WTB, which allowed WTB to collect on their notes. The UVTA can be valuable in remedying situations where one substantially reduces their net worth.

Appendix A

6. The debtor absconded

An absconding debtor is the next fraud indicator. An absconding debtor is someone who owes money to another person, and either runs away or goes into hiding to avoid being found by the person. There are very few recent cases of a debtor absconding after a fraudulent transfer, perhaps because in our modern era it is not so easy to go into hiding. However, the case of *In re Thomas*[9] from 1912 is illustrative of this principle.

John Thomas ran a horse stable in Utica, NY. His wife assisted him with the horse stable, and frequently acted on his behalf. While running the business, John became severely indebted to many creditors. He owed $255 to one creditor for horse carriages. More importantly, he had chattel mortgages on horses worth over $6,000. After becoming this indebted, John left Utica for New York City. He took some horses with him and sold them. After John had left, his creditors devised a plan to convert his assets into cash and distribute the proceeds amongst themselves. The creditors held an auction, sold some of John's assets, and collected more than $7,300 from the sale. John's wife acted as the auctioneer in her husband's absence. The United States District Court for the Northern District of New York enjoined the auction, and the creditors challenged the ruling.

One issue the court looked at was John's fraudulent intent. After reviewing the facts, the court found that John did in fact abscond. The court determined that John knew he was insolvent, he removed some of his assets when he fled to New York City, and he refused to pay back any of his creditors.

However, the court ultimately upheld the injunction of the sale of John's assets, and found certain creditors, who were trying to collect ahead of other creditors, guilty of conversion. Equity requires clean hands, and even creditors will not benefit from improper collection activities.

The Law of Fraudulent Transfers

7. The debtor removed or concealed assets

The seventh badge of fraud is where the debtor removed or concealed assets. As is common with the other badges of fraud, these occur when a debtor is facing serious legal issues. One interesting case illustrating this scenario is *United States v. Osborne.*[10]

Ileana Osborne was a real estate developer who worked on the Florida panhandle. In 2004, Ileana and another real estate developer started a real estate scheme to commit bank fraud. They would use a straw buyer to obtain a mortgage well above the home's asking price. After paying the closing costs and a kickback to the straw buyer, Ileana and her partner would pocket the difference and assume the payments for the mortgage. Then, they would let the mortgage default. After two years, the banks had over $29 million in losses. In 2006, one of the buyers sued Ileana and her partner, and the court entered a $1.7 million judgment against her. After this suit, Ileana was on the FBI's radar as a person of interest in a mortgage fraud scheme.

In 2012, Ileana obtained a divorce from her husband. During the divorce, Ileana transferred an interest in a civil lawsuit worth $120,000 to her husband, putting that sum out of reach from any creditors. Ileana's legal troubles were only beginning. In 2013, federal prosecutors charged Ileana with 45 counts of bank fraud. Ileana was sentenced to 32 months' imprisonment, and had to pay over $29 million in restitution. Four days later, she executed a quitclaim deed that transferred her home to her ex-husband for $100.

In 2016, Ileana and her husband faced yet another lawsuit. Here, the U.S. alleged that Ileana fraudulently transferred her home and her interest in the lawsuit to her ex-husband. After the U.S. filed a motion for summary judgment, the United States District Court for the Northern District of Ohio granted the motion on both counts. Ileana appealed.

On appeal, the Sixth Circuit Court of Appeals looked at a federal statute which listed the eleven non-exhaustive factors to determine whether the debtor had a fraudulent intent in making the transfer. With regards to Ileana's home transfer, the court found that such transfer was

Appendix A

fraudulent and concealed. In fact, the district court judge noted that he was deceived by the quitclaim deed transfer. However, the court denied the district court's grant of summary judgment on this count due to disputed issues of fact. With regards to the litigation rights, the court found that Ileana's transfer of the rights to her husband was both fraudulent and concealed from creditors. The court affirmed the district court's grant of summary judgment on this count and set aside the transfer of litigation rights. Under the UVTA, concealing such transfers is never a good idea.

8. The value of consideration received by the debtor was not reasonably equivalent to the value of the asset transferred or the amount of the obligation incurred

Evidence of fraud is found where the debtor did not receive a reasonably equivalent value to the asset transferred or the amount of the obligation incurred. Here, the courts need to determine whether the debtor received a consideration of reasonably equivalent value. If the debtor did not receive adequate consideration in exchange for the transfer, the transfer will be deemed fraudulent. A common fact pattern of this badge arises where one person makes a transfer of real property after being threatened with suit, as seen in *Mark Twain Kansas City Bank v. Riccardi*.[11]

James Riccardi was a businessman who owned stock in two corporations with his wife. One corporation was a Ford dealership, and the other one was a real estate holding company that held title to one property. In 1991, James, his wife, and the corporations experienced financial trouble. Mark Twain, a bank in Kansas City, Missouri, had a judgment worth more than $950,000 against both corporations and the Riccardis. A month after James was served, the property was conveyed from the real estate holding company to James' son, Gerald. Then, 29 days after the conveyance, a default judgment was entered in favor of Mark Twain by the Circuit Court of Jackson County. The defendants appealed.

On appeal, the Missouri Court of Appeals reviewed several badges of fraud to determine whether the conveyance of the property to Gerald was fraudulent. Both Gerald and his brother worked at the Ford dealership that their father owned. At trial, Gerald claimed that he received the property in exchange for receiving a lesser salary than his brother. However, after reviewing the other circumstantial evidence from the case, the trial court disregarded Gerald's testimony. Like the trial court, the appellate court found that Gerald received no concurrent consideration when the property was conveyed to himself from the real estate holding company. In addition to finding other badges of fraud, the appellate court affirmed the judgment of the trial court and held that the conveyance to Gerald was fraudulent.

Mark Twain was allowed to collect their judgment. Receiving something of reasonably equivalent value is crucial when parties consummate these types of transactions.

9. The debtor was insolvent or became insolvent shortly after the transfer was made or the obligation incurred

A debtor's insolvency around the time of the transfer or the incurred obligation can be a sign of fraud. Many of these fact patterns arise where the debtor becomes delinquent on loan payments, thus owing a significant amount to the bank. One case that deals with this issue is *Clark v. Bank of Bentonville*.[12]

Jack Clark owned a piece of property in Benton County, Arkansas that was financed by the Bank of Bentonville. In 1985, Jack became delinquent on his loans, and owed the bank over $190,000 in promissory notes. Once Jack's indebtedness came to the bank's attention, the bank sent a representative to meet with Jack, where they discussed alternatives to resolve Jack's delinquency. Jack offered to consent to a deficiency equaling the accrued interest on the loans, which the bank rejected. As a response to the rejection, Jack set up a trust in 1986 and conveyed the property into it. Jack's son was named as the trustee.

After the transfer, the bank filed a foreclosure action in the Benton County Chancery Court and obtained a deficiency judgment worth over

Appendix A

$190,000. In 1987, the bank filed suit to set aside the transfer as a fraudulent conveyance. The chancery court held the transfer to be fraudulent, and Jack appealed the district court's ruling.

On appeal, the Arkansas Supreme Court reviewed the record to determine whether the transfer of Jack's property into the trust was actually fraudulent. After Jack transferred the property into the trust, he did not have enough assets to make any more payments to the bank. Jack's conveyance of the property into the trust was also made after the bank made demands of him. In addition, Jack gave an insufficient consideration of $1 to his son, the trustee, when conveying the property into the trust. Jack was insolvent after the conveyance was made into the trust. People do not normally become voluntarily insolvent. After reviewing the record, the Arkansas Supreme Court affirmed the trial court and deemed the transfer to be fraudulent. The bank collected their $190,000 judgment. Becoming insolvent after making these transfers is something that does not go unnoticed under the UVTA.

10. The transfer occurred shortly before or shortly after a substantial debt was incurred

A transfer arising before or after a big debt obligation is the next insignia of fraud. An illustrative case regarding this badge is *Com. Bank of Lebanon v. Halladale A Corp.*[13]

Harold Mahan was a Missouri resident who owned a primary residence, two tracts of land, and a corporation named Halladale A. Corp. To cover Harold's expenses, he obtained four loans from Commerce Bank in 1974. Harold fell behind on his payments, and the bank made attempts to secure payment of the loans. Threatened with action from the bank, Harold made a few transfers in August of 1975. First, Harold deeded his primary residence and two tracts of land into Halladale. In turn, Halladale then issued 6,899 shares of stock to both Harold and his wife. Harold then set up a trust and named his son as trustee. Harold then transferred the 6,899 shares of Halladale into the trust, attempting to put everything out of reach from the bank. Harold and his wife died the following year in 1976.

In 1977, the bank filed an action in the Circuit Court of Laclede County to collect on the four loans, naming the two administrators of the estate as defendants. The bank obtained a judgment of over $28,000. The judgment, however, remained unsatisfied. Later that year, the bank filed a second action against several defendants, including Harold's surviving children, Harold's son as trustee of the trust, and Halladale. The circuit court found all the transfers to be fraudulent, and the defendants appealed.

On appeal, the Missouri Court of Appeals had the task of determining whether the transfers were improper. Fortunately, the court had 276 pages of exhibits on hand to make its determination that the transfers were, in fact, fraudulent. These exhibits pointed to several determinative facts. Almost all the property owned by Harold and his wife was transferred into the trust. Both of them had incurred substantial debts during the last two years of their life. They continued to live at their primary residence when the property was conveyed to Halladale. Most importantly, all of these actions were done after the bank reached out to Harold to secure the loan payments. The Missouri Court of Appeals had no trouble coming to its conclusion and affirmed the trial court's holding that the transfers were fraudulent. This allowed the bank to collect on their judgment. Making these transfers after going into debt is something the UVTA is equipped to address.

11. The debtor transferred the essential assets of the business to a lienor that transferred the assets to an insider of the debtor

The eleventh and final badge of fraud is where the debtor transferred the essential assets of the business to a lienor that transferred the assets to an insider of a debtor. These types of transfers allow the debtor, the lienor, and the insider to cut off any claims that an unsecured creditor may have

Appendix A

against the debtor. One example of this type of transfer is seen in *Northern Pacific Railway Co. v. Boyd*, which dates back to 1913.[14]

In 1886, the Coeur D'Alene Railroad & Navigation Company constructed a 33-mile-long railroad in Northern Idaho. Boyd worked on the construction of this railroad. In 1888, the president of the Coeur D'Alene Railroad entered into a contract to sell his stock to the Northern Pacific Railroad. Eight years later, in 1896, the Northern Pacific Rail*road* was bought out by the Northern Pacific Rail*way* (italics used for clarification). At the time of this sale, the Coeur D'Alene Railroad was still in existence. However, in 1899, the Northern Pacific Rail*way* bought Coeur D'Alene in a foreclosure proceeding.

After all of these acquisitions, Boyd still had not collected for the work done on the Coeur D'Alene Railroad. In 1898, Boyd filed suit against Coeur D'Alene and obtained a judgment for over $71,000. An appeal was taken but was ultimately dismissed. Boyd then brought suit in Idaho District Court against both the Northern Pacific Rail*road* and the Northern Pacific Rail*way* companies, claiming that both were liable on the debt owed by the former Coeur D'Alene Railroad. The case was removed to the United States Circuit Court in Washington. The circuit court held in favor of Boyd, and a lien was placed on the railway. The circuit court of appeals affirmed. The case was then appealed to the United States Supreme Court.

The Supreme Court determined the issue of whether Boyd could place a lien on the property of the railroad. The court noted that after all the transfers, Boyd was still not able to collect on his judgment of $71,000. Although there were many transfers involved, when the Rail*way* bought the Rail*road*, the Rail*way* was encumbered by the same debts that were originally assumed by the Rail*road*. Because of this assumption of liability, the court determined that Boyd was still entitled to be paid his $71,000 from the Rail*road*. The United States Supreme Court affirmed the Circuit Court of Appeals, and Boyd's lien on the railroad worth $71,000 was upheld. Although these situations involve complex fact patterns, the court was still able to reach an equitable solution.

Conclusion

As demonstrated by the eleven cases, the UVTA's badges of fraud have provided courts with guidance to successfully set aside a broad range of transfers. These indicators have prevented debtors from transferring environmental liabilities, corporate liabilities, homes, and other valuable assets into trusts, corporations, and to insiders. Creditors have benefitted as a result. However, the badges of fraud still have several issues that need to be addressed.

Will the law be amended to provide more definite contours to better guide courts? The UVTA encompasses a complex area of the law. Having some sort of limitations on what constitutes a fraudulent transfer will ameliorate the risk of producing inequitable results.

Will the UVTA's badges of fraud need to be amended to better set aside future transactions?

There are many different mediums available for debtors to store valuable assets. One such place is on a cryptocurrency exchange. Some recent cases involve a debtor attempting to transfer misappropriated assets into a cryptocurrency account to shield them from creditors.[15] Given the rising popularity of cryptocurrency, these transfers will only become more ubiquitous.

Or better yet, will court intervention even be necessary to void fraudulent transfers? There are new methods of vetoing transfers without any judicial oversight. Blockchain is one of these methods. Blockchain is a new technology which is used to both identify and prevent fraudulent transactions from occurring. In fact, some cases have already mentioned the use of blockchain technology to eliminate fraudulent transactions.[16] Given its rise in popularity, it is highly likely that blockchain will be used more frequently to preclude many fraudulent transfers well before a creditor files suit.

Appendix A

Fraudulent transfer law has already undergone three major changes in the last 110 years. It will need to undergo another change in the 21st century. This will ensure that the law is up to date, provides even better guidance for courts and attorneys, and produces the most equitable result for debtors and creditors alike.

Under the UVTA, the time to bring a claim may vary depending on the type of transfer. If the debtor has an intent to hinder, delay, or defraud a creditor, a creditor can bring a cause of action either within 4 years after the transfer or within one year after the transfer was or could reasonably have been discovered. If the debtor does not receive a reasonably equivalent value from the transfer, a creditor can bring a claim within 4 years after the transfer was made. If the creditor had a claim before the debtor either made the transfer to an insider or the debtor was insolvent at the time of the transfer, a creditor can bring a cause of action within one year after the transfer was made. While the time to bring a claim under the UVTA varies by transfer, the statute of limitations to bring a claim also vary amongst the different states.

Appendix B

Nevada Fiduciary Duty Law

**NRS 78.138 - Directors and officers:
Fiduciary duties; exercise of powers;
performance of duties; presumptions and considerations;
liability to corporation, stockholders and creditors.**

1. The fiduciary duties of directors and officers are to exercise their respective powers in good faith and with a view to the interests of the corporation.
2. In exercising their respective powers, directors and officers may, and are entitled to, rely on information, opinions, reports, books of account or statements, including financial statements and otherfinancial data, that are prepared or presented by:

    (a) One or more directors, officers or employees of the corporation reasonably believed to be reliable and competent in the matters prepared or presented;

    (b) Counsel, public accountants, financial advisers, valuation advisers, investment bankers or other persons as to matters reasonably believed to be within the preparer's or presenter's professional or expert competence; or

    (c) A committee on which the director or officer relying thereon does not serve, established in accordance with NRS 78.125, as to matters within the committee's designated authority and matters onwhich the committee is reasonably believed to merit confidence, but a director or officer is not entitled to rely on such information, opinions, reports, books of account orstatements if the director or officer has knowledge concerning the matter in question that would cause reliance thereon to be unwarranted.

Appendix B

3. Except as otherwise provided in subsection 1 of NRS 78.139, directors and officers, in deciding uponmatters of business, are presumed to act in good faith, on an informed basis and with a view to the interests of the corporation. A director or officer is not individually liable for damages as a result of an act or failure to act in his or her capacity as a director or officer except as described in subsection 7.

4. Directors and officers, in exercising their respective powers with a view to the interests of thecorporation, may:

   (a) Consider all relevant facts, circumstances, contingencies or constituencies, including, withoutlimitation:

   (1) The interests of the corporation's employees, suppliers, creditors or customers;

   (2) The economy of the State or Nation;

   (3) The interests of the community or of society;

   (4) The long-term or short-term interests of the corporation, including the possibility that these interestsmay be best served by the continued independence of the corporation; or

   (5) The long-term or short-term interests of the corporation's stockholders, including the possibility thatthese interests may be best served by the continued independence of the corporation.

   (b) Consider or assign weight to the interests of any particular person or group, or to any other relevantfacts, circumstances, contingencies or constituencies.

5. Directors and officers are not required to consider, as a dominant factor, the effect of a proposedcorporate action upon any particular group or constituency having an interest in the corporation.

6. The provisions of subsections 4 and 5 do not create or authorize any causes of action against thecorporation or its directors or officers.

7. Except as otherwise provided in NRS 35.230, 90.660, 91.250, 452.200, 452.270, 668.045 and 694A.030, or unless the articles of incorporation or an amendment thereto, in each case filed on or after October 1, 2003, provide for greater individual liability, a director or officer is not individually liable tothe corporation or its stockholders or creditors for

Nevada Statutory Law

any damages as a result of any act or failure to act in his or her capacity as a director or officer unless:

(a) The presumption established by subsection 3 has been rebutted; and

(b) It is proven that:

    (1) The director's or officer's act or failure to act constituted a breach of his or her fiduciary duties as adirector or officer; and

    (2) Such breach involved intentional misconduct, fraud or a knowing violation of law.

8. This section applies to all cases, circumstances and matters, including, without limitation, any change or potential change in control of the corporation unless otherwise provided in the articles of incorporation or an amendment thereto.

Appendix C

Corporate Dissolution

Statutes of Limitation

1. <u>Florida statute of limitation for corporate dissolutions</u>.

In Florida, the applicable limitation is referred to, not as a statute of limitation, but rather as a corporate survival statute. *See, Williams v. Clark Sand co., Inc.*, 212 So.2d 804, 806-07 (Miss. 2015) ("The Florida state at issue here is Section 607.1407. This statute, which tracks the Model Business Corporation Act Section 14.07, is a corporate-survival statute and is similar to the statutes adopted in numerous other jurisdictions.").

Fla.Stat. § 607.1406 pertains to "[k]nown claims against dissolved corporation."

Fla.Stat. § 607.1406, pertaining to "[u]nknown claims against dissolved corporation," provides:

"(1) <u>A dissolved corporation or successor entity may execute one of the following procedures to resolve payment of unknown claims</u>:

"(a) <u>A dissolved corporation or successor entity may file notice of its dissolution with the department on the form prescribed by the department and request that persons having claims against the corporation which are not known to the corporation or successor entity present them in accordance with the notice</u>. The notice must:

"1. State the name of the corporation and the date of dissolution;

"2. Describe the information that must be included in a claim and provide a mailing address to which the claim may be sent; and

Appendix C

"3. State that a claim against the corporation under this subsection is barred unless a proceeding to enforce the claim is commenced within 4 years after the filing of the notice.

"(b) <u>A dissolved corporation or successor entity may, within 10 days after filing articles of dissolution with the department, publish a "Notice of Corporate Dissolution."</u> The notice must appear once a week for 2 consecutive weeks in a newspaper of general circulation in the county in the state in which the corporation has its principal office, if any, or, if none, in a county in the state in which the corporation owns real or personal property. Such newspaper shall meet the requirements as are prescribed by law for such purposes. The notice must:

"1. State the name of the corporation and the date of dissolution;

"2. Describe the information that must be included in a claim and provide a mailing address to which the claim may be sent; and

"3. State that a claim against the corporation under this subsection is barred unless a proceeding to enforce the claim is commenced within 4 years after the date of the second consecutive weekly publication of the notice.

"(2) <u>If the dissolved corporation or successor entity complies with paragraph (1)(a) or paragraph (1)(b), **the claim of each of the following claimants is barred unless the claimant commences a proceeding to enforce the claim against the dissolved corporation within 4 years after the date of filing the notice with the department or the date of the second consecutive weekly publication, as applicable:**</u>

"(a) A claimant who did not receive written notice under s. 617.1408(9), or whose claim is not provided for under s. 617.1408(10), regardless of whether such claim is based on an event occurring before or after the effective date of dissolution.

Corporate Dissolution

"(b) A claimant whose claim was timely sent to the dissolved corporation but on which no action was taken.

"(3) A claim may be entered under this section:

"(a) Against the dissolved corporation, to the extent of its undistributed assets; or

"(b) If the assets have been distributed in liquidation, against a member of the dissolved corporation to the extent of such member's pro rata share of the claim or the corporate assets distributed to such member in liquidation, whichever is less; however, the aggregate liability of any member of a dissolved corporation may not exceed the amount distributed to the member in dissolution." (Emphasis and bolding added.)

Therefore, the Florida statute of limitation for corporate dissolutions generally is <u>four years after the date of filing the notice with the department or the date of the second consecutive weekly publication, as applicable.</u>

2. <u>New York statute of limitation for corporate dissolutions.</u>
New York has strict rules for the voluntary dissolution of corporations that are set forth in N.Y. Bus. Corp. Law §§ 1001-1009.
N.Y. Bus. Corp. Law § 1007, pertaining to "[n]otice to creditors; filing or barring claims," provides:

"(a) <u>At any time after dissolution, the corporation may give a notice requiring all creditors and claimants, including any with unliquidated or contingent claims and any with whom the corporation has unfulfilled contracts, to present their claims in writing and in detail at a specified place and by a specified day,</u> **<u>which shall not be less than six months after the first publication of such notice</u>**. Such notice shall be published at least once a week for two successive weeks in a newspaper of general circulation in the county in which the office of the corporation was located at the date of dissolution. On or before the date of the first publication of such

Appendix C

notice, the corporation shall mail a copy thereof, postage prepaid and addressed to his last known address, to each person believed to be a creditor of or claimant against the corporation whose name and address are known to or can with due diligence be ascertained by the corporation. The giving of such notice shall not constitute a recognition that any person is a proper creditor or claimant, and shall not revive or make valid, or operate as a recognition of the validity of, or a waiver of any defense or counterclaim in respect of any claim against the corporation, its assets, directors, officers or shareholders, which has been barred by any statute of limitations or become invalid by any cause, or in respect of which the corporation, its directors, officers or shareholders, has any defense or counterclaim.

"(b) Any claims which shall have been filed as provided in such notice and which shall be disputed by the corporation may be submitted for determination to the supreme court under section 1008 (Jurisdiction of supreme court to supervise dissolution and liquidation). A claim filed by the trustee or paying agent for the holders of bonds or coupons shall have the same effect as if filed by the holder of any such bond or coupon. <u>Any person whose claim is, at the date of the first publication of such notice, barred by any statute of limitations is not a creditor or claimant entitled to any notice under this section or section 1008.</u> **<u>The claim of any such person and all other claims which are not timely filed as provided in such notice</u>** <u>except claims which are the subject of litigation on the date of the first publication of such notice, and all claims which are so filed but are disallowed by the court under section 1008,</u> **<u>shall be forever barred as against the corporation, its assets, directors, officers and shareholders</u>**, except to such extent, if any, as the court may allow them against any remaining assets of the corporation in the case of a creditor who shows satisfactory reason for his failure to file his claim as so provided. If the court requires a further notice under section 1008, any reference to a notice in this section shall, to the extent

Corporate Dissolution

that the court so orders, mean such further notice, except that a claim which has been filed in accordance with a notice under this section need not be refiled under such further notice.

"(c) Notwithstanding this section and section 1008, tax claims and other claims of this state, of the United States and of the department of finance of the city of New York shall not be required to be filed under those sections, and such claims shall not be barred because not so filed, and distribution of the assets of the corporation, or any part thereof, may be deferred until determination of any such claims.

"(d) Laborer's wages shall be preferred claims and entitled to payment before any other creditors out of the assets of the corporation in excess of valid prior liens or encumbrances."

Therefore, the New York statute of limitation for corporate dissolutions generally is <u>not less than six months after the first publication of notice of dissolution to creditors and claimants</u>.

3. <u>Ohio statute of limitation for corporate dissolutions</u>.
Ohio.Rev.Code § 1701.87, pertaining to "[n]otice of dissolution; publication," provides:

"(A) <u>A corporation shall give notice of a dissolution by certified or registered mail, return receipt requested, to each known creditor and to each person that has a claim against the corporation, including claims that are conditional, unmatured, or contingent upon the occurrence or nonoccurrence of future events</u>.

"(B) <u>The notice shall state all of the following</u>:

"(1) That all claims shall be presented in writing and shall identify the claimant and contain sufficient information to reasonably inform the corporation of the substance of the claim;

"(2) The mailing address to which the person must send the claim;

Appendix C

"(3) **The deadline, which shall be not less than sixty days after the date the notice is given, by which the corporation must receive the claim**;

"(4) **That the claim will be barred if the corporation does not receive the claim by the deadline**;

"(5) That the corporation may make distributions to other creditors or claimants, including distributions to shareholders of the corporation, without further notice to the claimant.

"(C) Giving any notice or making any offer under this chapter shall not revive any claim then barred or constitute acknowledgment by the corporation that any person to whom the corporation sent notice under this section is a proper claimant and shall not operate as a waiver of any defense or counterclaim.

"(D) A claim is barred if a claimant that was given written notice under division (A) of this section does not deliver the claim to the dissolved corporation by the deadline stated in the notice.

"(E) The corporation shall post the notice described in division (B) of this section on any web site the corporation maintains in the corporation's name and shall provide a copy of the notice to the secretary of state to be posted on the web site maintained by the secretary of state in accordance with division (F) of this section.

"(F)(1) Except as provided in division (F)(2) of this section, the secretary of state shall make both of the following available to the public in a format that is searchable, viewable, and accessible through the internet:

"(a) A list of all domestic corporations that have filed a certificate of dissolution or have had their articles canceled;

"(b) For each dissolved corporation on the list described in division (F)(1)(a) of this section, a copy of both the certificate of dissolution and the notice delivered under division (B) of this section.

Corporate Dissolution

"(2) After the materials relating to any dissolved or canceled corporation have been posted for five years, the secretary of state may remove from the web site the information that the secretary posted pursuant to division (F)(1) of this section that relates to that corporation.

"(G) If the certificate of dissolution is filed five years or less after the effective date of this amendment, the corporation shall publish the notice described in division (B) of this section at least once a week for two successive weeks, in a newspaper published and of general circulation in the county in which the principal office of the corporation was to be or is located." (Emphasis and bolding added.)

In *SMS Financial 30, L.L.C. v. Frederick D. Harris, M.D., Inc.*, 112 N.E.3d 395, 402-03 (Ohio. App. 2018), the Ohio Court of Appeals recently concluded that the weight of evidence demonstrated that the notice of dissolution of a corporate borrower that was sent to a lender complied with Ohio. Rev. Code § 1701.87, where the borrower's attorney testified that he sent the notice by regular and certified mail; that the notice stated that all claims were to be presented in writing, identify the claimant, and contain sufficient information on the substance of the claim; that the notice stated the mailing address to use for claims, the deadline for receipt of claims, and that claims not received by the deadline would be barred; and that the notice advised that the corporation could make distributions to other creditors or claimants without further notice to claimant.

Therefore, the Ohio statute of limitation for corporate dissolutions generally is a given deadline <u>not less than sixty days after the date of the notice of dissolution by which the corporation must receive the claim</u>.

Appendix C

4. <u>Colorado statute of limitation for corporate dissolutions</u>.
Colo.Rev.Code § 7-90-912, pertaining to "[d]isposition of claims by publication," provides:

> "(1) <u>A dissolved domestic entity may publish notice of its dissolution and request that persons with claims against the dissolved domestic entity present them in accordance with the notice.</u>

> "(2) <u>The notice contemplated in subsection (1) of this section shall</u>:

> "(a) Be published one time in a newspaper of general circulation in the county in this state in which the street address of the dissolved domestic entity's principal office is or was last located or, if the dissolved domestic entity has not had a principal office in this state, in the county in which the street address of its registered agent is or was last located; and

> "(b) <u>State that, unless sooner barred by any other statute limiting actions, any claim against the dissolved entity will be barred if an action to enforce the claim is not commenced within five years after the publication of the notice or within four months after the claim arises, whichever is later</u>. The notice may contain such other information as the dissolved entity determines to include, including information regarding procedures facilitating the processing of claims against the dissolved entity; except that no obligations on persons having claims against the dissolved entity shall be imposed or implied that do not exist at law.

> "(3) <u>If the dissolved domestic entity publishes a notice in accordance with subsection (2) of this section, then, unless sooner barred under section 7-90-911 or under any other statute limiting actions, the claim of any person against the dissolved domestic entity is</u> **<u>barred unless the person commences an action to enforce the claim within five years after the publication date of the notice or within four months after the claim arises, whichever is later</u>**.

Corporate Dissolution

"(4) For purposes of this section and except where permitted to be disposed of under section 7-90-911, 'claim' means any claim, excluding claims of this state, whether known, due or to become due, absolute or contingent, liquidated or unliquidated, founded on contract, tort, or other legal basis, or otherwise. For purposes of this section, an action to enforce a claim includes an arbitration under any agreement for binding arbitration between the dissolved domestic entity and the person making the claim and includes a civil action.

"(5) This section shall not apply to a claim with respect to which notice has been delivered by a dissolved domestic entity under section 7-90-911 [pertaining to "[d]isposition of known claims by notification]." (Emphasis and bolding added.)

Therefore, the Colorado statute of limitation for corporate dissolutions generally is <u>within five years after the publication date of the notice or within four months after the claim arises, whichever is later.</u>

Appendix D

The Laya Factors
Laya v. Erin Homes, Inc.
177 W. Va. 343 (1986)

"Piercing the corporate veil" is an equitable remedy, the propriety of which must be examined on an *ad hoc* basis. *See* 1 W.Fletcher, *Cyclopedia of the Law of Private Corporations* § 41.25 (rev.perm.ed. 1983). "[D]ecisions to look beyond, inside and through corporate facades must be made case-by-case, with particular attention to factual details." *Southern Electrical Supply Co. v. Raleigh Country National Bank,* 320 S. E. 2d 515,523 (1984).

Some of the factors to be considered in deciding whether to pierce the veil are:

(1) Commingling of funds and other assets of the corporation with those of the individual shareholders;

(2) Diversion of the corporation's funds or assets to noncorporate uses (to the personal uses of the corporation's shareholders);

(3) Failure to maintain the corporate formalities necessary for the issuance of or subscription to the corporation's stock, such as formal approval of the stock issue by the board of directors;

(4) An individual shareholder representing to persons outside the corporation that he or she is personally liable for these debts or other obligations of the corporation;

(5) Failure to maintain corporate minutes or adequate corporate records;

(6) Identical equitable ownership in two entities;

Appendix D

(7) Identity of the directors and officers of two entities who are responsible for supervision and management (a partnership or sole proprietorship and corporation owned and managed by the same parties)

(8) Failure to adequately capitalize a corporation for the reasonable risks of the corporate undertaking;

(9) Absence of separately held corporate assets;

(10) Use of a corporation as a mere shell or conduit to operate a single venture or some particular aspect of the business of an individual or another corporation;

(11) Sole ownership of all the stock by one individual or member of a single family;

(12) Use of the same office or business location by the corporation and its individual shareholder(s);

(13) Employment of the same employees or attorney by the corporation and its shareholder(s);

(14) Concealment or misrepresentation of the identity of the ownership, management or financial interests in the corporation, and concealment of personal business activities of the shareholders (sole shareholders do not reveal the association with a corporation, which makes loans to them without adequate security);

(15) Disregard of legal formalities and failure to maintain proper arm's length relationships among related entities;

(16) Use of a corporate entity as a conduit to procure labor, services or merchandise for another person or entity;

(17) Diversion of corporate assets from the corporation by or to a stockholder or other person or entity to the detriment of creditors, or the manipulation of assets and liabilities between entities to concentrate the assets in one and the liabilities in another.

Laya v. Erin Homes, Inc. 177 W. Va. 343 (1986)

(18) Contracting by the corporation with another person with the intent to avoid the risk of nonperformance by use of the corporate entity; or the use of a corporation as a subterfuge or illegal transactions;

(19) The formation and use of the corporation to assume the existing liabilities of another person or entity.

Foot Notes

1. *Mark Fairchild "The 1770 Indian Famine and the American Revolution"*, AmericanSystemNow.com, October 5, 2018, https://americansystemnow.com/the-1770-indian-famine-and-the-american-revolution/

2. Victor I. Iles, *The East India Company, 1600-1774, and its Relation to the American Revolution,* (Kansas: University of Kansas, Lawrence 1905)

3. Iles, *The East India Company*

4. Iles, *The East India Company*

5. Iles, *The East India Company*

6. *Santa Clara v. Southern Pacific*, 118 U.S. 394 (1886)

7. 558 U.S. 310 (2010)

8. *People's Pleasure Park Co. v. Rohled*, 109 Va. 439, 61 S.E. 794 (1908) aff'd on reh'g, 109 Va. 439, 63 S.E. 981 (1909)

9. *Walkovszky v. Carlton*, 223 N.E.2d 6 (N.Y. 1966). The plaintiff was awarded $10,000, which is equivalent to about $85,000 in today's dollars.

10. Stephen M. Bainbridge and M. Todd Henderson, *Limited Liability: A Legal and Economic Analysis* (Northhampton, MA: Edward Elgar Publishing, Inc., 2016)

11. *United States v. Milwaukee Refrigerator Transit Co.*, 142 F. 247, 255 (E.D.Wis. 1905)

12. *Associated Vendors, Inc. v. Oakland Meat Co.*, 26 Cal.Rptr. 806 (Cal. App. 1962) (Commentators refer to the Associated Vendors list. We prefer the grittier defendant's name.)

13. 161 N.C. 35, 76 S.E. 533 (1912)

14. C.M.A. McCauliff, *Burdens of Proof : Degrees of Belief, Quanta of Evidence, or Constitutional Guarantees?* 35 Vanderbilt Law Review 1293,1328 (1982)

15. Jonathan Macey and Joshua Mitts, *Finding Order in the Morass: The Three Real Justifications for Piercing the Corporate Veil,* 100 Cornell L. Rev. 99, 109 (2014)

16. This case is based in part on *Bravo v. 2536-38 North Broad St. Assocs. LP*, Phila.ct Pl. Lexis 226 (2017)

17. *In re: eBay Inc. Shareholders Litigation* 29 Del.J. Corp. Law 924 (2004)

18. *In re: Tufts Electronics Inc.* 746 F2d 915 (1984)

19. This case is based in part upon *Chur v. Eighth Judicial Dist. Court of Nevada* 458 P3d 336 (2020)

20. *Guzman v. Johnson*, 137 Nev. Adv. Op.13 (2021)

21. *In re Hickory Printing Group Inc.*, W.D. North Carolina, 469 BR 623 (2021)

22. *Wallop Canyon Ranch, LLC v Goodwyn* 351 P.3d 943 (Wyo 2015)

23. This case is based upon *Big Sky Civil and Environmental v. Dunlay,* 429 P. 3d 258 (2018)

24. William L. Prosser, *Interstate Publication,* 51 Michigan Law Review 959, 971 (1953)

25. *McDermott, Inc. v. Lewis,* 531 A2d 206 (Del. 1987)

26. *Cort v. Ash* 422 U.S. 66 (1975)

27. This case, again using fictional names, is based in part upon a 2016 unpublished opinion arising out of the California Court of Appeals.

28. *Galvan v. Leake* No.03-15-00376-CV Texas Ct of App. (2016)

29. *Austin Powder v. McCullough* 216 A.D.2d 825 (New York 1995)

30. *Lunneborg v. My Fun Life* 431P.3d 187 (Idaho 2018)

31. 35 Cal. App. 4th 980 (1995)

32. *Angelo Tommasso Inc. v. Armor Construction and Paving, Inc.* 447 A2d 406 (Conn.1982)

33. *Conn. Light & Power Co. v. Westview Carlton Group*, LLC 950 A 2d 522 (Conn. 2008)

34. *Wachovia Securities, LLC v. Banco PanAmericano* 674 F 3d 743 (Ill. 2012)

35. *In Re Advanced Custom Builders,* LLC 2011 WL 3608004 (Iowa 2011)

36. *Tradewinds Airlines, Inc. v. Soros* 101 F. Supp3d 270 (New York 2012)

37. *CR Trust, Inc. v. First Flight LP* 580 SE 2d 803 (Va. 2003)

38. *LFC Marketing Group, Inc. v. Loomis* 8 P3d 841 (Nev.2000)

39. *Jamieson v. Jamieson* 2020 ONSC 6935

40. *Colandrea v Colandrea* 401 A2d 480 (Md 1979)

41. *Frazier v. Bryon Memorial Hospital* 775 P2d 281(Okla.1989)

42. *Shisgal v. Brown,* 21 A.D.3d 845 (N.Y. 2005)

43. *Las Palmas Associates v. Las Palmas Center Associates* 235 Cal App 3d 1249 (Cal.1991)

44. This case is partly based on *In Re Guava, LLC* 2015 Minn App Unpub LEXIS 826.

45. *Simplicity Pattern v. Miami Tru- Color* 210 A.D. 2d 24 (NY 1994)

46. *Peetoom v. Swanson* 778 N.E.2d 291 (Ill.2002)

47. *In Re Barnett v IRS* 988 F.2d 1449 (1993)

48. 748 F. 2d 1568 (1984)

49. 352 SE 2d 93 (W.Va.1986)

Appendix A
Foot Notes

1. Edward T. Wahl, *Fraudulent Transfers and the Uniform Fraudulent Transfer Act: An Overview,* 2009 WL 2510912

2. Unif. Voidable Transactions Act § 4 (2014).

3. *Matter of Reininger-Bone,* 79 B.R. 53,55 (Bankr. M.D. Fla. 1987).

4. *Slone v. Lassiter (In re Grove-Merritt),* 406 B.R. 7788 (Bankr. S. D. Ohio 2009)

5. *Tronox Inc. v Kerr McGee Corp. (In re Tronox Inc.),* 503 B.R. 239 (Bankr. S.D.N.Y. 2013)

6. *Taylor v. Rupp (In Re Taylor), 133 F.3d 1336* (10th Cir. 1998).

7. *Breitenstine v. Breitenstine,* 62 P.3d 587 (Wyo. 2003).

8. *Wash. Trust Bank v. Erickson,* 2012 Ida. Dist. LEXIS 58 Idaho Dist. Ct. 2012).

9. *In re Thomas,* 199 F.214 (N.D.N.Y. 1912).

10. *U.S. v. Osborne,* 807 Fed. Appx. 511 (6th Cir. 2020) (unpublished).

11. *Mark Twain Kansas City Bank v. Riccardi,* 865 S.W.2d 425 (Mo. App. W. Dist. 1993)

12. *Clark v. Bank of Bentonville,* 824 S.W.2d 358 (Ark. 1992).

13. *Com. Bank of Lebanon v. Halladale A Corp.,* 618 S.W.2d 288 (Mo. App. S. Dist. 1981).

14. *N. Pac. R. Co. v. Boyd,* 228 U.S. 482 (1913).

15. *Odyssey Reinsurance Co. v. Nagby,* 2019 U.S. Dist. LEXIS 223664 (S.D. Cal. Dec. 30, 2019).

16. *United Am. Corp. v. Bitmain, Inc.,* 2021 U.S. Dist. LEXIS 69525 (S.D. Fla. Mar. 31,2021).

Index

alter ego 9, 32-35, 41-42, 93-98, 100,101, 105-107, 124, 128, 130, 133,162,182

American Revolution 1-6

annual filings 179-180

Articles of Dissolution 150

bankruptcy fraud 121-122

bankruptcy trustee 57-58, 66-68

Business Judgment Rule 50, 59, 61-68

C corporation 17

CERCLA 154-155

certification 89-92

choice of law 85-86

Commenda II

commingling 101, 159, 167, 180-182

conflict of laws 86

contract piercing 19-20

corporate formalities 8, 29, 34, 42-43, 47 63, 83, 96, 102, 156, 165-182

corporate opportunities 53-60

corporate status 177

corporate veil 9, 18-19 41-43, 112, 165-167

corporate veil chart 8

corporation 10, 11, 15-17

debtor's prison 23

default judgment 80

dissolution 141-151, 213-221

dividends 50, 177-178

duty of care and loyalty 49-52, 53, 55, 59-60, 62

East India Company 1-5, 12-14

entity shielding 16

ESG 43

fiduciary duty 47-52, 55, 58, 63, 67, 77, 209

financial autonomy 183-184

fraudulent transfers 31-32, 193-208

government piercings 153-156, 162

Instrumentality Test 32, 35, 38-39, 41-42, 109-115

intercompany agreements 184-186

interlocking directors 52

internal affairs doctrine 86-92

international piercing 157-163

King George III 1-5

land trust 42-43

limited liability 11, 16-17, 23-24, 25-28

LLC 17-18, 24-25

LP 18,70

management issues 99-104

management separation 188-189

manager managed 169-171

member managed 169-171

minutes 175-176

non owner liability 103-104

nonprofit corporation 18

Oakland Meat list 29-32, 94-95, 166

organizational meetings 171-173

parent liability 137- 138

payroll taxes 153-154

perculium 10-11

personal guarantees 82, 110-112, 128

pierce the veil 41-42, 75-76, 82, 83, 100 , 103, 107, 122, 123-124,134, 145, 146, 167, 183, 189, 191

receiver 63, 66, 113

record retention 186-188

resident agent 174

reverse piercing 10, 127-131

S corporation 17

self-dealing 68-78

shareholder derivative suits 59, 72-73, 76-77

signs of sovereignty 189

Single Enterprise Theory 32, 39, 41-42, 139,
   189
sister entities 138-139
Sister Frankenstein 39, 42, 139, 183, 189
standards of proof 39-40
statute of limitations 146-151, 187
summary judgment 79-82, 123
Superman 33-35, 41, 93-98

tort piercing 20-21

unclean hands 108
undercapitalization 31, 117-125, 162, 178
Uniform Fraudulent Transfer Act 32,
   193-208

veil piercing standards 29-32
venue 85

Wizard of Oz 35-39, 42, 109, 115
Wyoming 24-25

About the Author

Garrett Sutton, Esq., is the bestselling author of *Start Your Own Corporation, Run Your Own Corporation, The ABC's of Getting Out of Debt, Writing Winning Business Plans, Buying and Selling a Business* and *The Loopholes of Real Estate* in Robert Kiyosaki's Rich Dad's Advisors series. Garrett has over thirty years' experience in assisting individuals and businesses to determine their appropriate corporate structure, limit their liability, protect their assets and advance their financial, personal and credit success goals.

Garrett and his law firm, Sutton Law Center, have offices in Reno, Nevada, and Jackson Hole, Wyoming. The firm represents many corporations, limited liability companies, limited partnerships and individuals in their real estate and business-related law matters, including incorporations, contracts, and ongoing business-related legal advice. The firm continues to accept new clients.

Garrett is also the owner of Corporate Direct, which since 1988 has provided affordable asset protection and corporate formation services. He is the author of *How to Use Limited Liability Companies and Limited Partnerships*, which further educates readers on the proper use of entities. Along with credit expert Gerri Detweiler, Garrett co-authored *Finance Your Own Business* and also assists entrepreneurs build business credit. Please see CorporateDirect.com for more information.

Garrett attended Colorado College and the University of California at Berkeley, where he received a B.S. in Business Administration in 1975. He graduated with a J.D. in 1978 from Hastings College of Law, the University of California's law school in San Francisco. He practiced law in San Francisco and Washington, D.C. before moving to Reno and the proximity of Lake Tahoe.

Garrett is a member of the State Bar of Nevada, the State Bar of California, and the American Bar Association. He has written numerous professional articles and has served on the Publication Committee of the State Bar of Nevada. He has appeared in the *Wall Street Journal, The New York Times* and other publications.

Garrett enjoys speaking with entrepreneurs and real estate investors on the advantages of forming business entities. He is a frequent lecturer for small business groups as well as the Rich Dad's Advisors series.

Garrett serves on the boards of the American Baseball Foundation, located in Birmingham, Alabama, and the Sierra Kids Foundation and Nevada Museum of Art, both based in Reno.

For more information on Garrett Sutton and Sutton Law Center, please visit his Web sites at www.CorporateDirect.com and www.Sutlaw.com.

How Can I Protect My Personal, Business and Real Estate Assets?

How Can I Clean Up My Entity to Strengthen the Corporate Veil?

For a free 15-minute consultation with an incorporating specialist call toll-free:
1-800-600-1760

For information on forming and maintaining corporations, limited liability companies and limited partnerships to protect your personal, business and real estate holdings in all 50 states visit the Corporate Direct website at:

www.CorporateDirect.com

Mention this book and receive a discount on your basic formation fee.

For more information about Garrett Sutton and his law firm visit www.sutlaw.com.

Other Books by
Garrett Sutton, Esq.

Start Your Own Corporation
Why the Rich Own their Own Companies and Everyone Else Works for Them

Writing Winning Business Plans
How to Prepare a Business Plan that Investors Will Want to Read – and Invest In

Buying and Selling a Business
How You Can Win in the Business Quadrant

The ABCs of Getting Out of Debt
Turn Bad Debt into Good Debt and Bad Credit into Good Credit

Run Your Own Corporation
How to Legally Operate and Properly Maintain Your Company into the Future

The Loopholes of Real Estate
Secrets of Successful Real Estate Investing

Scam-Proof Your Assets
Guarding Against Widespread Deception

Veil Not Fail
Protecting Your Personal Assets from Business Attacks

• • • • • • • • • • • • •

How to Use Limited Liability Companies & Limited Partnerships
Getting the Most Out of Your Legal Structure
(a SuccessDNA book)

Finance Your Own Business
Get on the Financing Fast Track
(a SuccessDNA book co-authored with Gerri Detweiler)

Toxic Client
Knowing and Avoiding Problem Customers